Single and Catholic

Judy Keane

Single and Catholic

Finding Meaning
in Your State of Life

SOPHIA INSTITUTE PRESS
Manchester, New Hampshire

Sophia Institute Press
Box 5284, Manchester, NH 03108
1-800-888-9344

www.SophiaInstitute.com

Sophia Institute Press® is a registered trademark of Sophia Institute.

Library of Congress Cataloging-in-Publication Data

Names: Keane, Judy, author.
Title: Single and Catholic : finding meaning in your state of life / Judy
    Keane.
Description: Manchester, New Hampshire : Sophia Institute Press, 2016. |
    Includes bibliographical references.
Identifiers: LCCN 2016012445 | ISBN 9781622822409 (pbk. : alk. paper)
Subjects: LCSH: Single people—Religious life. | Single people—Sexual
    behavior. | Catholic Church—Doctrines.
Classification: LCC BX2373.S55 K43 2016 | DDC 248.4/82—dc23 LC record
available at http://lccn.loc.gov/2016012445

First printing

Contents

Preface

About a year ago and almost immediately following a broken engagement, nothing could have surprised me more than the call I received from my editor at *Catholic Exchange*, who asked me, "Would you be interested in writing a book for Sophia Institute Press about being Catholic and single?"

Not the first post-breakup plan I had in mind. However, I realized that I was tremendously interested and certainly felt qualified to address the subject, given all of my firsthand experience! Then there was the timing. There is nothing like a full-time job and an eight-month book deadline to get your mind off a failed relationship and the plunge back into singlehood. I had to acknowledge, yet again, that God always has a plan as well as an amazing sense of humor!

From the beginning of this project, I knew only one thing for sure; I wanted this book to be about *all* Catholic singles, not just those starting to date. I have been around long enough to experience the many stages one goes through as a single, and I also know well the many complexities, circumstances, and struggles of the single life of others. Therefore, this is about all of us: those who are just starting out, those who have never married, those who have survived broken relationships, those who have not lived according to the Church but are considering and even try-ing to find their way back, and those facing single life once again because they have been widowed or are dealing with a separation or divorce. If this was to be a book for Catholic singles, it had to be for all of us who are out there on the front lines, trying to find our way; and especially about how we find our way as spiritual beings while managing everything on our own.

Having been single all my life, I can certainly draw from my own experience in many situations, but there are circumstances and challenges I have not faced, and I am grateful to the many singles who shared their circumstances with me. Consequently, I knew how important it was to include the needs and concerns of those who have endured the pain of a failed marriage and who may be going through the annulment process or struggling with the point of seeking an annulment. I hope that this book also addresses the struggles of those who suddenly find themselves single once again after the death of a beloved spouse as well as the very difficult trials of single parents, courageously raising children on their own.

It was a great gift to me, during a difficult time, to explore what it is to be Catholic and single and why it is more impor-tant than ever to live our Faith. I hope you too will come to a greater appreciation of our Faith and the opportunity we all have in seeking this path as well as embracing, with courage and tenacity, what it takes to live according to the truths to which we are called. It is something that Flannery O'Conner, a well-known Catholic, and single, fiction writer, knew well, saying, "The Truth does not change according to our ability to stomach it."

Single Catholics make up almost 40 percent of the Church. We may be single but according to those numbers, we are

Preface

definitely not alone! We are a diverse group and are single due to numerous circumstances, but we share many of the same challenges, and so we have a lot to offer each other. Therefore, I particularly wanted to talk to other singles and hear their stories along with what they have learned. Based on conversations and interviews I had with singles of all ages from across the United States and from various backgrounds and situations, I am able to share the stories of how other single Catholics are finding their way. I also thought it was imperative to hear from our spiritual leaders and to share their concerns and advice for Catholic singles who are under their pastoral care and are a significant percentage of the flock.

I invite my fellow Catholic singles to join me in considering where we are in our journey and to consider the possibilities and opportunities we have when we live by our Faith. Our Faith can help us figure out how to be alone without being lonely and can enable us to recognize that God's grace is greater than anything life can throw at us. I also want to acknowledge how much *is thrown* at us as singles, especially these days.

I hope to emphasize the power we have individually and collectively to be a profound and positive influence in the Church as well as in the hookup world we live in. I want to encourage you through the stories of many others like yourselves in this book, to realize that you are not really alone and to explore the countless positive ways in which we can take care of ourselves physically, emotionally, and spiritually while supporting each other and those around us.

It is also my hope that this book will remind you that you are unrepeatable, irreplaceable, and uniquely special and that your life is about experiencing each moment as it comes rather than anticipating how it will all turn out.

Single and Catholic

I can't guarantee you that by reading this book, your prince or princess will come to rescue you. Nor can I assure you that loneliness and struggle will no longer be a challenge. But I hope you will be inspired to recognize what your present life can be and realize how important and extraordinary it is for you to be seeking another way to live. Above all, you will learn that you are not alone on this journey.

If you are a practicing Catholic single or are thinking of coming back to the Church after some time away, or even if you are simply looking for greater meaning and more substantive answers in response to the confusing messages of our time, then this book was written for you.

—Judy Keane

Acknowledgments

There are always people who contribute to the completion of any book, whether it is through their encouragement, their prayers, their insight, or their advice. Consequently, I would like to thank the following individuals whose contributions have helped me enormously throughout this project.

I am deeply indebted to Michael J. Lichens, my editor at *Catholic Exchange* and at Sophia Institute Press, who initially approached me with the wonderful idea of writing a book specifically for Catholic singles, about the challenges we face in the world today. I am grateful for his discerning feedback and unwavering support throughout this project. I am also grateful to Sophia Institute Press for giving me the opportunity to write a book explicitly meant to support and encourage Catholic singles everywhere and to remind us that we do not walk alone in these times when the spiritual stakes have never been higher.

I am especially grateful to the Most Reverend Thomas J. Olmsted, bishop in my home Diocese of Phoenix, Arizona. Despite his very demanding calendar, Bishop Olmstead was generous with his time, his excellent counsel, and his willingness and enthusiasm in allowing me to share his pastoral advice for Catholic singles. In addition, Bishop Olmsted also shared invaluable guidance regarding discernment of God's plan for our lives.

I am also deeply indebted to His Excellency Robert D. Gruss, bishop of Rapid City, South Dakota, for graciously taking time out of his very busy schedule to share his personal story and his awareness of the challenges Catholic singles contend with today. I am particularly grateful for Bishop Gruss's unique perspective and wisdom on this subject because it is grounded in his own extended time as a Catholic single before his priesthood. His insight resulted in one of the most significant and inspiring quotes in this book.

In addition, I am very grateful for the invaluable help of the many devout priests who shared their concerns and support for Catholic singles in our Church today. Particularly, I would like to thank Father Donald Calloway, vocation director of the Marians of the Immaculate Conception; Father David Konderla, pastor of St. Mary's Catholic Center at Texas A&M University; Father Paul Sullivan, director of vocations for the Diocese of Phoenix; and Father Michael Lightner, parish administrator for St. Margaret Mary Catholic Church and School in Milwaukee, Wisconsin. You will find their significant insights and contributions throughout this book.

I also want to thank my dear friend of over twenty years, Ann Fairbanks, for her tremendous generosity, encouragement, and support. Her feedback, expansive vocabulary, and editor's eye have been invaluable to me in writing this book.

Words are inadequate to express how deeply indebted I am to the many amazing Catholic singles I was blessed to meet throughout the writing of this book. A crucial part of this book was your valuable input. Your insight and your experience emphasize how much we all have in common. By your words and

Acknowledgments

by your life, you effectively convey that we are single but are not alone. Most importantly, each one of you witnessed to the joy that can be found in living our Catholic Faith and how important it is to "keep on keeping on," from wherever you are in seeking God in your lives. The courage and conviction each of you shared reaffirms that it is possible to grow spiritually, and live faithfully, during these times that can be disheartening for many of us.

Beyond this, I am deeply grateful to my mother, Janet, who not only gave me the great gift of my Faith, but also taught the Faith each day through her deep devotion and acts of kindness. I would also like to thank my cherished sisters, Nancy and Liz, for their love, encouragement, and enthusiasm throughout this project.

Finally, please know how grateful I am to so many of you who offered your prayer support as I worked to complete this book. Your prayers and love assisted me more than you'll ever know.

Generally, when we find ourselves doing something that was the last thing we had planned to do, God is at work in our lives. I thank God and my Church for everything that led me to the writing of this book and for His graces that were evident throughout the process.

Once again, God had a much better plan for me than I had for myself, just as He does for all of us.

Single and Catholic

1

Living the Single Life with Passion and Dedication

There is no point in sugarcoating it. Living the single life — and choosing to live it according to our Catholic Faith — is not easy. There are times when we wonder if there is anyone else out there like us, other single Catholics who are faced with the same temptations, frustrations, loneliness, and challenges. Regardless of whether it is by happenstance or by choice, living life as a single has its unique challenges. And the difficulty is compounded when we are people of Faith while our culture is decidedly not.

Remember the famous line "You complete me" from the film *Jerry Maguire*? It can seem romantic to think that a love interest will complete us as people, but we are already complete — and becoming more so in God's plan. I know for a fact that God doesn't build us halfway. It's not as though we arrive here as half of a matched set, half a soul, wandering the world as an incomplete being because we have not met our spouse. Yet we live in a society that can make us feel as if romantic love and marriage is the only way to feel whole.

Well-meaning relatives often tell us to "find someone to settle down with — and soon!" If only it were that easy! Has it ever seemed to you that, as single adults, there seems to be a perception that we are in a sort of time warp, exiled in the desert of singleness until we are granted a reprieve in a happily-ever-after wedding? Perhaps we too might feel that life will really begin only when we find our true love or when we decide firmly for religious or consecrated life. In our single state, we all have experienced how frequently assumptions are made and labels are applied. Because I am a single Catholic who is no longer in her thirties and has not yet married, others assume that I have decided not to marry and have children. This could not be further from the truth! In my case, it is not by choice. Simply put, it has not happened yet.

How Many Single Catholics Are There?

There are millions of Catholic singles out there. If you combine the numbers from the 2014 General Social Survey[1] (religious affiliation and marital status) released by National Opinion Research Center (NORC), based at the University of Chicago, along with the most recent numbers from the U.S. Census Bureau's American Communities Survey[2] (population data), it is estimated there are 8.1 million never-married Catholic men (ages eighteen and older) and 8.8 million never-married Catholic women (ages eighteen and older) living in the United States.

If you add to these totals Catholics who have divorced (annulled or not annulled) and widowed Catholics who have not

[1] Michael Hout and Tom W. Smith, *Fewer Americans Affiliate with Organized Religions, Belief and Practice Unchanged: Key Findings from the 2014 General Social Survey* (Chicago: NORC, 2014), last modified March 10, 2015, accessed July 14, 2015, http://www.norc.org/PDFs/GSS%20Reports/GSS_Religion_2014.pdf.
[2] "Population Estimates," United States Census Bureau, accessed July 6, 2014, http://www.census.gov/popest/data/counties/totals/2014/index.html.

remarried, the numbers increase to approximately 11.7 million single Catholic men and 15.1 million single Catholic women in the United States.

Because of the current culture of cohabitation, casual sex, and serial dating, combined with a high divorce rate and a tough economy, high student-loan debts, and high unemployment, there is now a trend of people waiting longer than ever to marry. According to the most recent data from the U.S. Census Bureau, there are 99.6 million unmarried people living in the United States! That is just over 43 percent—nearly half of all U.S. residents eighteen and older. Unlike those generations who lived at home until they married in their early twenties, the vast majority of adults are now living on their own prior to tying the knot. Further findings from the U.S. Census Bureau[3] also estimated that 45 percent of all households nationwide are being maintained by unmarried men and women.

This phenomenon is not limited to the United States. The business research firm Euromonitor International has found a growing global trend of single people living alone.[4] Across the globe, the number of one-person households has risen by 30 percent over the last ten years. Euromonitor International's list of factors contributing to this global trend include increased standards of living, a growing tendency for young people to focus more on their education and careers, and the rise of global female employment and the growing ability for women to support

[3] Ibid.
[4] An Hodgson, "One Person Households: Opportunities for Consumer Goods Companies," Euromonitor International, September 27, 2007, accessed July 14, 2015, http://blog.euromonitor.com/2007/09/one-person-households-opportunities-for-consumer-goods-companies.html.

themselves. Finally, among an aging population, the loss of a spouse can often results in many older adults living alone.

The Good News about Being Single

Here is the good news: statistically singles today are actually more active in serving the community than our wedded counterparts, and our Faith can help us to reach out to others. I hope it will come as no surprise that, married or not, we are all happier when we are practicing our Faith. According to a recent Gallup Healthways Well-Being Index derived from interviews conducted in 2010 and 2011, Americans who describe themselves as "most religious" have the highest levels of well-being. And we all know that serving others and the Church leads to a greater sense of peace. As single people, we can embrace the call of our Catholic Faith in new and unique ways.

The statistics I've given can seem daunting, but there are some great moments of encouragement we should take from them. Look back on those statistics and realize these three things: first, there are millions of us single people out there in the world making an impact — for "better or worse." Second, there is greater fulfillment and happiness when we practice our Faith. Third, on a global scale, we are staying single longer for a variety of reasons. We're not alone, and we're certainly doing more than waiting for our future spouse.

When we look at the statistics and consider our own experience, we see that Catholic singles are a large and diverse part of Christ's Body. We are college students and cab drivers, teachers and techies, cattle ranchers and corporate professionals, physicians and philanthropists. We strive to live our single lives with dignity, passion, and dedication, as our Faith calls us to nothing less. We serve our communities and our country. We may be divorced and annulled, raising our kids as single parents; we may be in college; we may be widows and widowers; we may be discerning our vocation; we may be consecrated laypersons; or we may still be searching for "the one." We share the common bond of singleness and are one in being with the Mystical Body of Christ—and a significant part of the universal Church.

We Have Opportunities That We Shouldn't Waste

Although many of us might still hope to marry, being single in a couples' world actually does come with perks. For one thing, our single state allows us to have more spontaneity than those who are married. This gives us a tremendous opportunity to do fun things such as travel to faraway lands or do something different at mealtimes. More importantly, it allows us to open ourselves in service to God and gives us the time to serve our Church and pursue our spirituality in a way that married people cannot. We are in a unique position to respond to God with the words "Speak, LORD, for thy servant hears" (1 Sam. 3:9). Our singleness allows us a certain freedom to "unfurl the sails, and let God steer us where He will."[5]

We must recognize that our lives are the lives we are living now! Our single state is an opportunity to say yes to God with complete abandon—truly to be open to whatever He might be calling us to. When we open ourselves to His will through prayer and complete commitment, we will see amazing changes take place in our lives.

Even going back to Christianity's very roots, we see that the Church and her saints have always seen the need for single people who can fully devote their life. Although our single state

---

[5] St. Bede, *The Age of Bede*, trans. J. F. Webb and D. H. Farmer (New York: Penguin Classics, 1998), 228.

may not be permanent, as it was for St. Paul and countless others, we are still in a unique place to do great works and fully devote ourselves to work and worship in a way that our married friends might find impossible. Rather than lament our lives as they are, and merely wait for what we want, we can seize this moment to do great things that will only bring us more joy and, if we are called, make us fantastic spouses!

Being single has its challenges, as does every station in life. Maybe you feel as if God has forgotten you or that He does not hear your prayers. In reality, though, God knows intimately the unique challenges of your single life, and He hears your prayers. Nobody knows your situation and what you long for better than our Father in Heaven, who watches over you 24-7!

It is important to take a moment to think of the many ways God has provided for you and protected you throughout your life. Think for a moment of how He has kept you on the straight and narrow or away from situations that would not have been best for you, even when His answers have been a simple no. If you are ever in doubt, read Psalm 139, which presents a magnificent portrait of His all-knowing love for you.

> O LORD, thou hast searched me and known me!
> Thou knowest when I sit down and when I rise up;
>   thou discernest my thoughts from afar.
> Thou searchest out my path and my lying down,
>   and art acquainted with all my ways.
> Even before a word is on my tongue,
>   lo, O LORD, thou knowest it altogether. (Ps. 139:1–4)

Whether you have been walking the single path of life for a while now or it has recently become part of your life, God knows that being on our own can also be something of deep value. For it to be of value, however, we must seek His presence in our lives and His will, especially through receiving the Eucharist and partaking of all His graces. He is also always to be found in Adoration and in the confessional. In fact, He is always just a prayer away, even in the privacy of our daily lives. God is called the "Father of the fatherless and the protector of widows" (Ps. 68:5), but we can see that He is also the comforting companion for those of us who remain single. Even if we feel alone, we are always honored guests in the House of the Lord.

Beyond our needs, we can be great supporters and intercessors for our family, our friends, our work colleagues, our country, and our world in its spiritual thirst. We singles are in a wonderful position to be witnesses and prayer warriors for Him in the here and now!

We are also called to be joyful, no matter what our vocation or state in life. Blessed Mother Teresa of Calcutta once aptly said that "joy is a net of love by which we can catch souls."[6] One of the greatest bearers of joy in our modern times is Pope Francis, who has remarked about the importance of committing to our Faith. Pope Francis emphasized that belonging to the Church is essential to being a Christian:

> There are those who believe you can have a personal, direct and immediate relationship with Jesus Christ outside of the communion and the mediation of the Church. These are dangerous and harmful temptations.... On the contrary, you cannot love God outside of the Church; you cannot be in communion with God without being so in the Church.[7]

---

[6] *Mother Teresa: Contemplative in the Heart of the World*, ed. Angelo Devananda (Ann Arbor, MI: Servant Publications, 1985), 61.
[7] Pope Francis, General Audience, July 25, 2014.

Single and Catholic

If you are like me, your reality is quite different from the reality you had hoped for or prayed about through the years. While I watched the vast majority of my friends marry, I found myself on a different path—one of protracted singlehood. But I have learned that this path is no less great. It is one filled with ongoing spiritual development, adventure, and amazing people. Of course, it's also a path where we can grow in love and gratitude for the goodness of God.

On my journey, I have been blessed to experience things I would not have experienced had I been married. I have lived in foreign lands and have been fortunate to see parts of the world that I might never have seen had things been different. I have been able to pursue a satisfying and demanding career. I have been politically active for my state and country and for the rights of the unborn; this would have been much more difficult to do if I had responsibilities at home and to a family. I have also had the opportunity to pursue my passion for writing, especially about the love I have for my Catholic Faith. Speaking only for myself, a single woman and a proud owner of three rescue cats, I still hope to find Mr. Right, but only God knows whether my path will bring me to marriage.

The only thing any single Catholic can be sure of right now is that we are called not to wait idly for that day. We are not to wait to live at all. Together, we will recognize that life is too fascinating and too short for us to be on standby.

As we journey through this book, you will hear from Catholic singles across the United States as well as Catholic clergy who offer practical advice and support for living life as a single Catholic today. It is my hope that you will find within each chapter words of encouragement and an understanding that you are not alone and that your role as a single in today's Church is essential—and much more.

2

Forgotten Catholics?

To those of us who are unmarried, the Church can seem like a place where we don't quite fit in. As one Catholic single put it to me, "The Church doesn't quite know what to do with us." Yet, according to a 2007 CARA study focusing on marriage in the United States, 47 percent of adult Catholics (ages eighteen and older) have either never married, or are divorced (includes annulled), widowed, or separated. The survey notes that 25 percent of Catholics have never married, 13 percent are divorced or separated, 5 percent are widowed, and 4 percent are living with a partner outside of marriage.[8] When you look at the numbers, it is evident that we are a sizable group! Unfortunately, the laudable focus of the Church on married couples and the family can sometimes make singles feel like outsiders when it comes to finding support within our parish communities. Given the significant number of U.S. Catholics who are single, it might be a good idea for Pope Francis to call for a synod on the single life!

---

[8] Mark M. Gray, Paul M. Perl, Tricia C. Bruce, *Marriage in the Catholic Church: A Survey of U.S. Catholics* (Washington, D.C.: Center for Applied Research in the Apostolate, 2007), 3.

Single and Catholic

For anyone who is single, divorced, or widowed for any length of time, the Church community can feel like a lonely place. After all, it's not easy sitting in the pews week after week alone and surrounded by married couples and families. Parishes do pray for those of us who are single in terms of discernment of religious life or for an increase of vocations to the married life, but rarely, if ever, do parish communities pray for the real-world challenges that today's singles face. This is not to say that there isn't a strong need to focus on the sanctification of the family, which is clearly under attack in our society. Unfortunately, there does not seem to be much out there for the rest of us living outside of marriage. Despite our large numbers, parish structures tend to place pastoral emphasis on married couples and families with children. Those of us who find ourselves "flying solo" often argue that there is little available within our parish ministries that speaks to our unique situations.

As Catholics living outside the married state, we too are on the front lines in trying to maintain our faith in a world that works relentlessly against Christ's teachings. As faithful singles finding our way in the secular world, we are regularly targeted and challenged with messages that strongly encourage us to find our happiness and fulfillment in ways contrary to the morals and values Jesus calls us to. In almost every respect, the secular world ridicules our beliefs and beckons us to turn our back on our Faith. It is the greatest danger that we face spiritually as Catholics. It should not be an unfounded hope, then, that Catholics who are single, separated, divorced, or widowed would look to the Church to find encouragement and support with regard to our plight "in going it alone" during these challenging times.

Consequently, it is imperative that the Church recognize the large and dynamic group that we are and consider the pastoral needs that exist among us. Just as married couples with problems in their relationship should be able to count on the assistance and guidance of the Church, so too should those living outside the state of marriage.

Thankfully, headway is being made in the Church regarding ministry to single Catholic parents as well as those who are separated, divorced, or contending with abusive marriages. According to the final document brought forth by the October 2014 synod of bishops on marriage and family, a two-week Vatican summit called for by Pope Francis to discuss the challenges of modern family life, "Respect needs to be primarily given to the suffering of those who have unjustly endured separation, divorce, abandonment, or those who have been forced by maltreatment from a husband or a wife to interrupt their life together." Along with emphasizing the necessity of addressing the consequences that separation or divorce have on children, the synod fathers also discussed the need for "special attention to be given in the guidance of single-parent families. Women [and men] in this situation ought to receive special assistance so they can bear the responsibility of providing a home and raising their children."[9]

As single women and men, we must also draw strength through the sacraments and through Adoration. But many of us find ourselves too old for young-adult ministry programs and yet way too young for senior support groups. Basically, there are a whole lot of us stuck in a vast empty middle ground devoid of Church programs that are relevant to our lives! So what are we, as Catholics

---

[9] *Relatio Synodi* of the III extraordinary general assembly of the synod of bishops: "Pastoral Challenges to the Family in the Context of Evangelization," October 5–19, 2014, 47.

who are not married, to do? It is important to realize that our faith in God that sustains us.

The Mass and the sacraments must be at the heart of who we are, along with Christ, who is and always will be our true fulfillment. We should not judge our Faith as lacking because of any perceived lack of support within our parish community. If we perceive a deficit of support, it is simply a need to be filled. And who better to fill it than those of us who see and feel the need! Although it is not always easy to do, it is up to each of us to step out and get involved or create Church activities that will connect us to each other according to the different types of support we seek. If you find that such programs aren't available at your local parish, consider discussing this with your pastor and finding like-minded singles to help initiate a program. In addition, you could look to other parishes and see what they are doing. We can also use the Internet to connect as Catholics, not simply as a pseudo Match.com, but to mobilize as Catholic singles in creating networks to mentor and support each other. Given our numbers and talents, we have the potential to do great things for our Church and each other if we come together. If you are simply seeking involvement, there are a number of national Catholic organizations or nonprofits that you can join.

By "putting myself out there" and following God's lead, I have met wonderful people who have become lifelong friends. Years ago, I joined a board that puts on a large annual Catholic conference. My work with this wonderful group of talented people has led to friendships that I still enjoy more than two decades later! Whatever volunteer work I've done, whether for a pro-life crisis pregnancy center, sitting on a committee within my diocese, or becoming an overseas aid worker, has enriched my life and helped me not only to serve Christ and His Church but also to meet others and have amazing experiences. So cast a wide net and don't be afraid of moving outside your comfort zone! It will lead you to feeling less isolated, and you will see the hand of God at work as He leads you to others who will support you and share in your struggles.

It is true that if we want to see change for us in the Church, it needs to begin with each of us. If you are divorced and looking for support, it may be up to you to start a divorced support group in your parish. If you are single and there are no single groups, then maybe it's time to start a Catholic meet-up group or a Theology on Tap evening. It will take creativity and dedication, but establishing networks in which we can look after each other will be our answer. Therefore, we must work with our local parishes to help drive the change we would like to see. Our priests and our religious, as well as the many hardworking lay ministers in the Church, carry a great burden and do their best to serve so many. So perhaps we can best serve our Church by serving each other.

3

Catholic Singles and Today's Dating Scene

As a single woman who feels called to the vocation of marriage, I still hold out hope that one day I will meet "the one" and be happily married. Throughout my life, I've had some wonderful relationships that did not lead to marriage but were positive experiences that taught me significant life lessons. I am grateful for those relationships. There were other relationships that left me perplexed, disappointed, or downright brokenhearted. Nonetheless, the lessons I learned from those experiences were also vital and, in many respects, even more important. It's all part of the trial-and-error world we singles call the dating scene.

While I remain optimistic about my future, married or not, I can say with confidence, as many of you also know — it's hard out there! Unfortunately, it's challenging enough finding someone we click with, much less finding someone who shares our Catholic convictions.

This chapter is not, however, about wallowing in self-pity or stressing out about our situation. It's about having hope for your future and making the most of your single state. If you truly feel called to the vocation of marriage, you must also have faith that God will bring that special person into your life. It should come as no surprise, though, that we must be prepared to accept that it might not happen in our desired time frame. Our Faith calls us to submit to the will of God in trust. There is added comfort in knowing that we are not alone. There are millions of other Catholic singles who share the same hopes and dreams and the same struggles and challenges that we have.

As we search for "the one," it is easy to get discouraged. When we are faced with these discouragements we have two options: we can either follow the promptings that seem to be coming from the Lord or give in to despair and settle. Before we go for that last option and settle, it's important to remember that the Lord will not prompt us to a dead end, nor will He guide us by despair. We are called to be faithful to Him and to grow in holiness. There are plenty of examples of those joyful weddings where single people have waited trustingly for the Lord.

Each of us is ultimately called to holiness, whether single, married, divorced, widowed, priest, or religious! When God is first in our lives, we will have healthier, happier, and holier re-lationships. When we allow God's grace to guide us in becoming the best version of ourselves, we are not likely to waste our time, or that of another, in a relationship without a future. Nor are we as likely to distract ourselves in ways that people do to fill their emptiness when they are not actively seeking God's will in their lives. Living according to God's grace will allow you to recognize the right person when God brings him or her into your life, and best of all, you will be worthy of that person.

Fall in Love with God First

We might be called to marriage or the religious life, but the single years are an important time to grow closer to God and better prepare ourselves for a future spouse or a religious vocation. In the single life, we are completely free to exercise who we are and to develop who we ought to be. This is truly a time of formation and learning from God in your alone time with Him.

The real-world challenges to dating include finding someone with the same drive for holiness of mind, body, and soul that you have. You cannot force a person to want to be holy. If you meet another Catholic who doesn't share your level of faith, you can only set the bar by how you live your own life. If that potential spouse jumps on the band wagon through your example, great! But if he doesn't, you should reevaluate whether this is going to be the best relationship for you. Before you even start to date again, try what my friend Lova suggests: Fall in love with God first!

Fall in love with doing God's will even if it's not exactly what you thought or dreamed it would be. Being single is just a status; it is not who we are, and it doesn't define us. Singlehood is a blessed journey of self-worth and self-discovery that is forming us into the men and women we will be for a future spouse or religious vocation. We are Catholic, and we are children of God, loved and thought of intensely by Him. So fall in love with saying yes to God's plan for you, just as Mary and Joseph did.

Like Lova and the rest of us who are no longer in our twenties, what do we do when we have the feeling that life is passing us by or even when we begin to question God's timing?

Patience and Prayer

Because "with God all things are possible" (Matt. 19:26), you just never know what will happen! One of my dearest friends happened to meet her husband while standing in line at a coffee shop. Another met her spouse through mutual friends who thought they just might be a match. Still another friend met his future wife after he decided to pop into the Adoration chapel one evening to say a few prayers. He noticed an attractive young lady praying, they spoke, and they now are blessed and happy in a sacramental marriage. Therefore, we have to forget the statistics and remain optimistic!

If we are looking for a spouse, prayer is certainly a key component in finding the right one. Through prayer, we will be more likely to hear and follow the desires God places in our hearts and be open to go wherever He may lead us. Regardless of when we discover our vocation, the journey we are on is worth traversing while we are making ourselves better people and better Catholics. One of the men I talked to, acclaimed author Joseph Pearce, was one of us who had to wait. Although he is a well-known author and critic, not many are aware that he met his wife relatively late in life.

Joseph and his wife would finally receive the sacrament of marriage when he was forty. For him, patience is the key virtue in the single life: "The only practical advice that I can offer is patience and prayer." This may seem simple, but prayer is what allows us to get to know God continually and to listen for His promptings of grace to go wherever He sends us. "The desire for marriage," Joseph told me, "must be animated and motivated by a desire to lay down our lives self-sacrificially for the beloved. For this desire to remain paramount in our hearts, we need to pray for grace."

After prayer, the old adage "God helps those who help themselves" comes to mind when considering what it takes these days to meet someone. There are the obvious ways—getting involved in hobbies and interests that appeal to us, networking through friends and family, joining professional associations or Catholic singles groups, volunteering, attending recreational organizations, mixers, and parties.

Although it certainly takes both optimism and courage to brave this generation's world of online dating, the Internet provides opportunities that deserve consideration. In a 2013 survey published in the *Journal Proceedings of the National Academy of Sciences*, 35 percent of 19,000 individuals who married between 2005 and 2012 met their life partner online. Additionally, the study found that approximately 45 percent of the couples in that sample met specifically on dating sites or through online social networks, chat rooms, instant messaging, or other online forums. Many of us have realized that we need to widen our opportunities beyond our parishes and local faith communities. Luckily, there is the option of a number of orthodox Catholic dating websites available for those of us hoping to find someone who shares our values (see the resources for a list of these sites).

Obviously, online dating has significant features to consider. First, it is very important to be honest with yourself when setting the parameters of a search and carefully considering what is realistic for you in respect to proximity, education, and background. It may seem as if these things do not matter, but if you have any experience at all in the dating world, you have already learned how important these issues can be. Second, be aware that the impersonal nature of this medium can tempt us into a "shopping" mentality that objectifies others, a practice that is clearly contrary to our Faith. Unquestionably, online dating is a tool to use with caution and consciousness.

It is also important to find out just what someone means when he says he is Catholic and how significant the teachings of his faith are to him. It is true that you could be the means of drawing someone deeper into his faith, but this is also a time to be responsibly discerning and careful that we are not hearing only what we want to hear. It is imperative that we are honest with ourselves and those we meet online. Honesty, integrity, and discernment are vital in this new dating medium, just as they are in all things.

However you approach dating, it's important to lay your cards on the table early in a relationship and not to be afraid to ask key questions within the first few dates to determine if you are a match. You may go out on dates with those who are seemingly Catholic but find out later that they are really cafeteria Catholics or don't prefer to adhere to Church teachings. Then there are those who are truly practicing their Faith, and you have to feel for where their heart truly is.

You can find great guidance on many Catholic dating websites that also provide in-depth views on Church teachings and Christian ideals that can help you stay mindful of "what is right" when searching online. Although online dating might not be for everyone, many couples have met and married through Catholic Internet communities, and it is a tool to consider. Assuredly, the majority of online participants would say they never thought they would be there either, but thank goodness they found the nerve because it is currently a viable means of meeting others with similar beliefs.

Whatever ways you pursue in trying to meet someone, it's important to ask yourself if you are taking the steps to meet someone. We can't expect our future just to open up and reveal itself with a spouse dropped off on our doorstep. If you're not sure of the next step, you can always start by getting involved in the Church. There you will grow in holiness while serving others and you'll be introduced to a wider variety of Catholics.

Nonetheless, it might be tempting to stay with someone who is not the best for us because it is better than being alone or simply because we are tired of looking and are willing to settle for "good enough." It's important, however, to examine the downside of that choice, which may inevitably lead to dangerous or unhealthy compromises. If the person we are seeing does not truly have our welfare at heart, that would prove that the person could not possibly be what God wants for us. Similarly, how can we have anyone's best interests in mind if we have concerns that the person is not right for us? Are we settling, rationalizing, or giving in to fear in any way in a relationship?

If you find you are settling, please consider that you are betraying yourself and the person you are with and at the same time eliminating any possibility of being available for the right relationship. No matter what, it is better to remain single than to settle.

Some dating relationships that we have high hopes for don't work out. They might appear promising at the start, leading us to believe that this is the person God means for us, but then they end in heartbreak. When things don't work out, what we perceive as God's no could, in retrospect, actually reflect the fact that we quit listening to God a while back in that relationship. If that is the case, it can serve as an important opportunity to learn from our mistakes and become stronger and clearer about what *is* right for us. God supports us in our heartbreak; He does not lead us to it.

It's also important to be mindful that God's no is to deter you from entering into a relationship or a lifetime commitment that could lead only to mediocrity and even misery. Listen to God, however He tries to reach you, often through your family and friends. If they have concerns, pay attention! What is the point of forcing things that are not good for you? If it is not good for you, it cannot possibly be good for the other person, no matter what that person might say. Relationships *can* be difficult, but they should not be difficult in a way that diminishes either of you.

Heartbreak can lead to despair, or it can challenge us to put our hope in God once again so He can make us stronger and wiser. If we respect ourselves and others, settling is not an option. Personal growth and spiritual growth in this area of our lives is necessary in order for us to become both a worthy human being and a worthy partner.

St. Teresa of Ávila once said, "There are more tears shed over answered prayers than over unanswered prayers." Looking back over my own life, I thank God that I didn't get certain jobs I wanted so badly and that certain relationships that I had hoped would work out ended instead. With 20/20 hindsight, I can see clearly how God's infinite wisdom was at work in what I had thought were unanswered prayers.

Obviously, if we are out there looking, we have to know what we do want in a partner as well as what we don't. Therefore, what should we look for in a future spouse? I'd like to share two pieces of advice I received from priests in my life: (1) marry someone who brings you closer to God; (2) look for someone who exhibits the seven gifts of the Holy Spirit: wisdom, understanding, knowledge, counsel, fortitude, piety, and fear of the Lord.

If you've dated for any length of time, you know that you always take risks when you open your heart to someone. Although we might sometimes find disappointment, it is in the searching that we might also find the love of our life. St. Thérèse of Lisieux gave us some of the best advice I have ever read, "At every moment do what Love requires." If you take that wisdom to heart and live it, and if you are earnestly seeking God's will and actively working to become the kind of person you want to attract into your life, you are on your way to finding love—and living fully while you're at it.

The important thing is to remember that, as with anything else in life, it takes prayer, work, and patience. Equally important is to live your life fully in the present, with integrity, passion, joy, and faith.

4

Myths and Misunderstandings about the Single Life

No matter how accomplished we might be as singles, we often deal with questions, statements, misunderstandings, unintentional insensitivity, and even, on occasion, overt prejudice in a couple-oriented world. Understandably, these myths and misunderstandings can give the message that we are somehow incomplete because we are not married. Inescapable questions such as "When are *you* getting married?" and "Do you have children?" as well as a variety of well-intentioned inquiries and advice may or may not become any easier to negotiate as we grow older.

Here are a few questions that might be familiar to you — followed by the implied judgment:

"Why aren't you married?" (What's wrong with you?)

"Can't you just find someone and settle down?" (You must be difficult to get along with.)

"Don't you want children?" (The clock's ticking!)

"Have you tried online dating?" (You are not trying hard enough.)

"The right person is not going to just come up and knock on your door" — followed by various suggestions regarding how to meet people.

"Do you think you're just being too picky?"—which brings us back to the overriding insinuation of "What's wrong with you?"

As singles, we've become used to contending with the implications of well-meant but insensitive questions that challenge us to remain charitable. An even greater challenge is listening graciously to the variations of "words of wisdom." For example, we have all heard, *way* too often, "It will happen when you least expect it." God should give great graces to every one of us who listens to this pearl with a straight face! Another one is that sometimes we are viewed as incomplete by others until we find our "other half." Unfortunately, it is unlikely that these kind souls understand how insulting this can be to us and how it can imply that we are not living a full and meaningful life already and are instead just letting time pass while anxiously waiting for someone to come along and *complete* us. On more than one occasion, it has been suggested to me by well-intentioned souls to pray, "St. Ann, St. Ann, send me a man, as fast as you can," which implies that being a single female is somehow a bad thing and therefore we should try to get this over with as soon as possible.

Those who hope to marry might also contend with the assumption from others that finding your future husband or wife should somehow be easy. And perhaps it would be easy if we were willing to marry just anyone for the sake of being able to say, "I'm married." As Catholics, however, we know the profound commitment that is involved when we enter into the sacrament of Marriage with the words "till death do us part." Therefore, finding the *right* someone is not as simple as marrying just anyone so we can join the ranks of the married.

Those of us wishing to marry will often find ourselves dealing with observers of our lives who assume that we aren't trying hard enough, that we are being too picky, or that we have unrealistic expectations. When we run into this, we have to remember that there is nothing wrong with trying to find a partner who is a practicing Catholic who not only shares our faith and values but whom we are attracted to and compatible with. If we were to do anything other than that, we would be untrue to ourselves and to God. Granted, inevitably there will be times when pursuing this worthy goal can feel like trying to find a white cat in a snowstorm!

Snap judgments must be particularly challenging for those who feel called by God to remain single or who feel content and at peace in serving the Church as a consecrated layperson. In these cases, questions about marriage are insensitive, and it is to be hoped that out of respect and support for your decision, others will spare you the typical comments and questions as you cope with the same myths that many singles face.

It can be particularly challenging once we move past the average marriageable age and find that others have a tendency to assume we've made the choice not to marry and have a family, when in fact, this may not be the case at all.

Bella DePaulo, PhD, a clinical professor of social psychology and author of the book *Singled Out: How Singles Are Stereotyped, Stigmatized, and Ignored, and Still Live Happily Ever After,* has dedicated much of her career to examining and correcting the mysths about singles and what she considers to be a widespread societal bias toward unmarried adults. According to DePaulo:

> If you tell new acquaintances that you are single, they often think they already know quite a lot about you. They understand your emotions: You are miserable and lonely and envious of couples. They know what motivates

you: More than anything else in the world, you want to become coupled. If you are a single person of a certain age, they also know why you are not coupled: You are commitment-phobic or too picky or have baggage. From knowing nothing more about you than your status as a single person, other people sometimes think they already know all about your family: You don't have one. They also know about the important person or persons in your life: You don't have anyone. In fact, they know all about your life. You don't have a life.[10]

It is important to consider that most of the people in our lives are coming from a place of love, concern, and authentic interest in our happiness, even if their questions and advice can seem hurtful or cause us to assume that until we meet "the one" we are somehow deficient. We have to figure out how to live with it, because it is unlikely that questions about our single status from well-meaning relatives or within social situations will stop anytime soon. The best way to prepare ourselves to deal graciously with the inevitable comment is to examine some of the more common myths and misunderstandings we encounter as singles.

Most importantly, we need to make sure we are not buying into these myths ourselves! We need to remember that God is calling us to particular vocation, which we'll explore later. Remember that our single state is not just a time of waiting but a time in which we seek out God and His plan for us. First, though, let's explore these myths.

---

[10] Bella DePaulo, *Singled Out: How Singles Are Stereotyped, Stigmatized, and Ignored, and Still Live Happily Ever After* (New York: St. Martin's Press, 2006), 3.

Myths and Misunderstandings

Myth 1: We are not complete until we are married.

Singles are frequently portrayed in the media as undatable losers crying into their beer, collecting cats, or eating ice cream by the pint while lamenting their lonely existence and lost dreams. To some extent we may also buy into this negative portrayal when we choose to believe in the myth that marriage will meet our deepest needs and that, once married, our lives will truly begin.

This fallacy is also supported by the assumption that if you are single, you are interested in only one thing—getting married! While many of us might wish to marry one day and might be taking active steps to do so, we must also be aware of the trap of seeing ourselves in a type of holding pattern until we finally tie the knot. Beyond this, we must also remain cognizant that our worth does not hinge on our marital status. St. Paul, a single man himself, recognized this and by his example calls us to discover the unique gifts we have in being single while also weighing carefully whether we have a vocation for marriage or the single life:

> I wish that all were as I myself am. But each has his own special gift from God, one of one kind and one of another. To the unmarried and the widows I say that it is well for them to remain single as I do. (1 Cor. 7:7–8)

Although the majority of people do marry, Paul points out that it is not necessarily God's will for everyone. Because Paul was not committed to the responsibilities of marriage, he was able to devote his life to spreading the Word of God according to God's plan for him. St. Paul says that some of us might also be called to remain single and that it is a good thing, since each situation has gifts in its own right. In 1 Corinthians, Paul speaks of the gifts that are part of being single:

I want you to be free from anxieties. The unmarried man is anxious about the affairs of the Lord, how to please the Lord; but the married man is anxious about worldly affairs, how to please his wife, and his interests are divided. And the unmarried woman or girl is anxious about the affairs of the Lord, how to be holy in body and spirit; but the married woman is anxious about worldly affairs, how to please her husband. I say this for your own benefit, not to lay any restraint upon you, but to promote good order and to secure your undivided devotion to the Lord. (1 Cor. 7:32–35)

As singles, our central responsibility is to discern the will of God in our lives, to be "about the affairs of the Lord" and also to embrace fully the situation in which we find ourselves. Therefore, it is good to prayerfully consider whether the option of remaining single may be what we are called to. Even if we are not called to a permanent single state, we can see our current situation as part of our greater vocation. Despite its unique challenges, it also has its rewards. No matter where we are in the discernment process, we are all called to grow in our Faith and live it fully in our lives. Unquestionably, if we hope to marry, we are also more likely to find the right person because we are seeking to live the right way.

Myth 2: We must compromise ourselves in order to find a spouse.

The greatest danger perpetuated by modern culture is that the morals and values of the Catholic faith are irrelevant. Consequently, we are told that we are completely out of touch with real life if we think that we can live up to those values and still hope to have a significant relationship and get married. This is one of Satan's most cunning and dangerous lies, and we are challenged daily not to buy into it. Regarding the reality of Satan and his deceptions, Pope Francis has said, "He presents things as if they were good, but his intention is destruction.... Satan has invented humanistic explanations that go against man, against humanity and against God."[11] Unfortunately, the consequence of the success of this lie is that we live in a world that is becoming more and more confused about the meaning of sex and love while denying there is even such a thing as sin.

Because of the prevailing cultural attitude that celibacy is almost abnormal, there is the pressure to lower our standards if we want to be in a relationship with anyone or to marry. There is also the tendency to embrace the rationalization that because something feels right, it is right. At times we feel tempted to question whether God's way is indeed the best way, as we see others living outside the demands of our Faith, marrying and having children, while we may see our own relationships end due to staying true to our beliefs. Simply put, the pressures and temptations that exist today are intense, and the impact they are having on our world has been so life changing that they can only be from the "father of lies" (John 8:44).

When we compromise our spiritual and moral values, however we may justify it, we are turning away from the great gift of our Faith and buying into the fallacy that since "everyone else is doing it," that somehow makes it okay. We can be tempted to

---

[11] Elise Harris, "Pope Francis: Satan Seduces by Disguising Evil as Good," Catholic News Agency, September 29, 2014, accessed July 17, 2015, http://www.catholicnewsagency.com/news/pope- francis-satan-seduces-by-disguising-evil-as-good-85265/.

think that marriage will solve a whole host of problems, including our desire for love, acceptance, and a sense of self-worth. If we truly wish to follow Christ, however, we must ask ourselves why we would consider compromising our beliefs to catch the eye or heart of another. Similarly, if a person who claims to love us is pressuring us to compromise ourselves and our values, we should ask ourselves if this is really someone we want to spend the rest of our lives with and if this is what we really think love is.

Tragically, there are many people who have given in to the pressure and the expectation that if we hope to marry, we must compromise our values from a sexual standpoint in order to "land" a partner or just to stop being alone. Many of our peers and the larger culture have lowered the bar on sexual morality, convinced that this is a less judgmental and rigid way to live. We also find pressure into accepting confusion, resentment, and disillusionment as normal and inevitable aspects of being in a relationship. If this is something you feel you have done too, know that you can always begin again.

In these challenging times, it has never been more imperative for those of us who cling to our Faith to remain true to our beliefs and rise to answer the challenge. Otherwise there is no hope. The assault on God's truth regarding sex, marriage, love, and the value of human life has escalated into an obvious war between good and evil in our world. In the singles world, those of us on the frontlines trying to live faithfully can send the message that God's way is not obsolete.

There are still many out there who continue to persevere. One of these is Jackie. An exceptionally beautiful and talented thirty-six-year old artist who runs her own art and interior-design company, Jackie is also a former third runner-up in the Miss Universe Canada Pageant. Beyond being a successful artist and businesswoman, she is deeply involved in the community affairs and philanthropic work of the large city where she lives. As someone who has been in serious relationships and is committed to remaining chaste until marriage, she offers this advice about the lies that Satan tells us and how we can combat them:

> The advice I would give to those who are influenced by such ways of thinking is not to believe the father of lies! Do not wait another second to throw yourself in the loving arms of our Lady, who eagerly waits to take you to our blessed Lord. With Him you will find peace that no one and nothing on earth can give you. Be brave and do not waste sufferings that come your way as a single person, but offer them to God. God *does* love you, and He *does* have a plan for you. Trust in Him! He knows best! I would also suggest finding a good priest or spiritual director to speak with and to stay close to the sacraments, especially going to Mass as often as possible, receiving Holy Communion, and going to Confession on a regular basis.

Admittedly, it can be discouraging to continue to meet people who expect you to compromise your values, only to see the relationship end because you are unwilling to do so. It still doesn't take away from the fact that time was spent in getting to know these people, even if you found out that on key issues you were not going to be a match. However, it is a good thing to have learned this before marriage. After all, isn't this the point of dating? It is understandable that there will be times that ongoing experiences such as these can leave us feeling disappointed, discouraged, and even hopeless.

Single and Catholic

Myth 3: Singles have a lot of time on their hands.

One of the most common myths associated with single life is that those who are single and who do not have children have lots of time on their hands. I would submit that many singles would agree this is definitely *not* the case! Many married couples may not really consider what life is like for singles, going it alone in respect to errands, laundry, cooking, groceries, housekeeping, and the multitude of other tasks that are just part of everyday living. For example, if our car should break down, we're on our own to find another ride. In addition, if we have the flu or are dealing with health concerns, we are likely to be our own caregivers. I recall an occasion when I cut my finger badly while preparing dinner. With no one to turn to, I had no choice but to drive myself to the nearest emergency room. Such are the realities of single life.

Another common misconception is that singles don't have as many commitments or extracurricular demands as couples do. Nothing could be further from the truth. Consider that in addition to everything else, we have to make the considerable time and find the energy to date while we cultivate relationships; all while working, taking care of ourselves, and possibly taking care of others, including aging parents.

The goal here is not to denigrate or criticize our married friends and family or to seek sympathy and pity. Rather, it is to explore the myths and the realities with which single Catholics live. Therefore, it is important to clarify that the sacrament of Marriage is "held in honor among all" (Heb. 13:4). And we certainly understand that marriage and family life have their own challenges.

Whether single or married, we all face the challenge to recognize that while we are all busy, we can't lose sight of what is most important in our lives: God and our Faith. One of Satan's

4

greatest tools is to use the world's distractions to keep us so busy that we no longer have time for God. It's easy to get caught up in all the external enticements the world offers while letting our Faith take a backseat. To avoid this, we must make a conscious decision to remain active in our spiritual lives.

"It is important to use our time well, and it is not something society helps us with," Bishop Thomas J. Olmsted of the Diocese of Phoenix told me. "We often have many things that are a terrible use of time." While contemplating advice, Bishop Olmsted considered that our time is our most important resource as single Catholics. When we consider our days and what we do to keep busy, perhaps there are things we can cut out and other activities we can take up that help to form us into better people. "So be aware that time is a gift from God and make an effort to discipline yourself in how you use time," Bishop Olmsted continues.

Although you might be feeling pressured and can't imagine where you'd make better use of your time, you'd be surprised at the ways you can use the time you have to build up yourself and your friends. Instead of watching a movie or catching up on a show, you can begin to read books that help you in your prayer and spiritual life. Instead of listening to music when you work out, you can listen to sermons, lectures, or audiobooks that make you into more of what you feel called to be. If you used every minute effectively, imagine how much more you'd also be able to talk about when you get those awkward questions about being single and when you'll get married.

Myth 4: After a certain age,
it is unlikely that a person will marry.

We're told that after a certain age, the odds are against those of us who would still like to be married. For those of us who are getting older and are still single, it's easy to buy into the myth that the chances are "slim to none" of finding someone who shares our Faith and with whom we are compatible. Certainly, we know there was a better chance of finding someone when we were younger. Nonetheless, we must remember that God tells us that with Him "all things are possible" (Matt. 19:26).

For the faithful, this can still be considered a myth despite any empirical evidence to the contrary. Those of us who are still hoping to marry must forget the statistics and remain hopeful, knowing that God can bring two people together under any circumstance and that He trumps every statistic that you might hear.

Several years ago, while I was working at a large and reputable health-care organization in Phoenix, I met a woman named Mary who had recently retired from her career as a high school teacher in the public school system. She was sixty years old, and in the course of our conversation, I found out that she had never married but always wished to. Since she was retired, she had come to the hospital to volunteer a few hours each week in order to remain active and give back after a successful career. A few months later, I met another hospital volunteer named Joel, a man in his late sixties, who had retired years earlier after a long and prolific career serving in the United States military. He told me about how he had lost his wife the year before and that he began volunteering at the hospital as a way to help him cope with his devastating loss. About a year later, Mary came into my office to tell me that she had some very exciting news. She and Joel had met months before while volunteering in the same department and were now engaged! I tell this incredible story to offer hope to anyone who might still wish to marry but feel that it is outside the realm of possibility. Mary and Joel are a great example of how God can work in bringing two people together in His good time when it is His will.

Myth 5: Those who do not marry will die alone.

Naturally, if we wish to marry, we might feel fearful at times that we will never find someone to share our lives with and that we will grow old and die alone. Yet how does getting married guarantee you won't die alone? Occasionally we hear amazing accounts of couples who have been married to each other for most of their lives and then die within days or sometimes within hours of each other. The fact is, however, that the majority of widows and widowers face years and sometimes decades on their own after their spouse dies. Such was the case for my own paternal grandmother, who was married to my grandfather for sixty-five years. My grandfather died in his early eighties, and my grandmother, who was a few years younger, spent the next two decades of her life as a widow, eventually passing away at ninety-nine years old. We still celebrate such stories but obviously, whether married or single, we may all face the challenge of living without a spouse. In this we are reminded, as in all things, that God's grace is what we must seek as our refuge, our strength, and our hope, no matter what circumstances we find ourselves in.

Additionally, even though we are single, it doesn't mean we don't have families or support. We can build these relationships in our lives just as married people work on their relationships. It is in caring for others that we will be cared for. In fact, as singles, we are more likely to reach out consistently to family members, relatives, and close friends to build bonds with those whom we are willing to help and who will be there for us too. Our Faith gives us the consolation that when we follow Jesus we are never alone and that He is with us throughout our lives and at the hour of our death. Thus, there is nothing to fear when we have faith in God.

There are other myths and misunderstandings we could discuss with regard to being single, but what is most important is to make sure we do not allow stereotyping and assumptions to get the best of us. Since we "know neither the day nor the hour" (Matt. 25:13) of when our earthly lives will end, it is important always to live in the present moment and remind ourselves daily that God's plan for our lives is always far better than ours and that heaven must always remain our constant and ultimate goal.

5

Saints for Singles

It's easy to get caught up in thinking that many answers to life's questions and quandaries can somehow be found online these days. Because we have a world of information at our fingertips, it seems obvious to use the information highway to seek all kinds of "advice" and "guidance." However, discernment is vital when traveling this road. With the technology available to us, it is easy forget about the world's greatest wireless connection: prayer!

Since long before the information age, Catholics have turned in prayer to the saints and asked for their intercession before the Trinity. The Communion of Saints includes those who can help us and can take our petitions to God. As Catholics, we believe that the saints in heaven remain in union with us on earth. Just as we might ask a family member or a friend for a favor, we can ask the saints for their assistance as we work to fulfill God's will in our lives.

The saints can be invaluable friends, as they know the difficulties and temptations we come across in our daily lives and are ready to help! Think for a moment about the magnitude of this gift in our lives. At any given moment, those great souls are willing and waiting to assist you in every facet of your life.

Single and Catholic

Church tradition teaches us to believe and trust this truth and make it a vital part of our spiritual lives.

There is perhaps no greater assurance of the saints' willingness to intercede for us than the words of St. Thérèse of Lisieux, the nineteenth-century saint who once said, "I want to spend my heaven doing good on earth."[12] Therefore, in this chapter, I will focus on saints specifically for singles, as well as suggested saints for those who are divorced or single parents. If you have not sought the saints' intercession in your faith life before, I encourage you to give it a chance and see what happens.

Mary, the Mother of God

There is no more powerful intercessor before the Holy Trinity than the Virgin Mary, the Mother of God and Queen of All Saints. We also recognize her as the Mother of the Church. Because of her maternal heart, Mary cannot remain indifferent to the needs of her earthly children and is the ideal saint for singles to approach in asking for her motherly guidance and intercession with all matters of life.

Because by her absolute *fiat* (Luke 1:38), Mary consented to the Incarnation, through which "the Word became flesh and dwelt among us" (John 1:14), we see why she holds a special place in the Church. Because of her yes, we can be confident that God the Father will never say no to anything she requests of Him. Because of the unity between Mary and her Son, she is also the best guide to Christ in never failing to draw us closer to Him through her prayers for us before the throne of God. The

---

[12] St. Thérèse of Lisieux, *The Final Conversations*, trans. John Clarke (Washington, D.C.: ICS, 1977), 102.

Catechism of the Catholic Church has this to say about Mary's ongoing motherly care for each of us on earth:

> "This motherhood of Mary in the order of grace continues uninterruptedly from the consent which she loyally gave at the Annunciation and which she sustained without wavering beneath the cross, until the eternal fulfillment of all the elect. Taken up to heaven she did not lay aside this saving office but by her manifold intercession continues to bring us the gifts of eternal salvation.... Therefore the Blessed Virgin is invoked in the Church under the titles of Advocate, Helper, Benefactress, and Mediatrix" [*Lumen Gentium* 62]. (CCC 969)

If you haven't tried praying to the Virgin Mary for her intercession, why not give her a chance to work in your life? Speak to her as you would speak to your mother, a trusted relative, or your best friend. Bring to her all that is weighing on your heart—from the big things to the little things, knowing that she will always bring them before her Son, who, in turn, will always grant what is best for you.

For such prayers to the Mother of God, we find a great and ancient prayer in the Holy Rosary. If you are unfamiliar with the Rosary, it is a simple form of meditative prayer that is prayed on a string of beads. Given to us by the Most Holy Virgin Mary, it is a powerful tool that can work wonders in your life as you offer your Rosary for various intentions.

If you are just starting to pray the Rosary, you may feel as if all you are doing is saying a bunch of prayers over and over. But at the heart of the Rosary is the spiritual edification you will receive in spending quiet time each day meditating on the lives of Jesus and Mary and the salvation history made possible because of them. Along with a focus on key events in the lives of Jesus and His Mother, the Rosary is an opportunity to pray for a variety of intentions, not only for ourselves and our families, but also for the Church, the world, and those who have gone before us.

Sister Lucia de Jesus dos Santos was one of the three shepherd children who witnessed a series of Church-approved apparitions of the Virgin Mary in Fátima, Portugal, in 1917. Prior to her death in 2005, Sister Lucia said that "the Most Holy Virgin in these last times in which we live has given a new efficacy to the recitation of the Rosary to such an extent that there is no problem, no matter how difficult it is, whether temporal or above all spiritual, in the personal life of each one of us, of our families ... that cannot be solved by the Rosary. There is no problem, I tell you, no matter how difficult it is, that we cannot resolve by the prayer of the holy Rosary."[13]

Although Mary was married to St. Joseph, whom we discuss below, she is still a Mother who wants to hear from us and to assist us with our challenges. In your daily prayers, perhaps this good Mother is the one to whom we need to bring the challenges of our single life. We can't be guaranteed that a wife or husband will be immediately given to us, but meditating on her faith, love, and devotion can make us better Christians in our daily life.

Our Lord could have entered the world in a multitude of ways, but he chose Mary to be His Mother. Let us honor Jesus' parting gift to us from the Cross — the gift of His own beloved Mother, given to the world to intercede for us so that we may gain eternal

---

[13] "The Rosary," The Fatima Message, accessed January 19, 2015, http://fatima.ageofmary.com/rosary/.

life and be with her Son forever (see John 19:26–27). Our Lord greatly honors and loves His Mother so much. Shouldn't we as well?

Saint Joseph

Because he is, among other things, the patron of real estate, St. Joseph is often associated with the long-standing Catholic devotion of burying a small statue of him upside down somewhere in a yard and praying for a quick home sale. But behind the sometimes perfunctory portrayal of Joseph as a heavenly real-estate agent is a great man who is recognized by the Church as being the ideal spouse and the ideal father. Despite his humble work as a carpenter, this descendant of royal lineage of the House of David remains the ideal model for Christian manhood and Christian fatherhood. We remember St. Joseph as the patron saint of workers, carpenters, fathers, and just the right man for us to contemplate while we live out the single life.

St. Joseph has an important message especially for men. In the Bible, we see him as a man of patience, courage, compassion, wisdom, and strength — in other words, the kind of man all Christian men are called to become. St. Joseph stands out as an exemplary role model not only because of his deep devotion to Mary and Jesus, but also because of his humble obedience in following so faithfully the will of God. Today he is popularly invoked as patron of the universal Church. With this title, he has been given charge over guiding and protecting the Church and all her members. Women hoping to marry can approach St. Joseph, the ideal husband, for help in their search for the right man. Similarly, single men hoping to marry can look to Joseph to help them be great husbands and great fathers.

I have benefitted from the powerful helping hand of St. Joseph many times in my life. I once explained to a friend that I had recently prayed a novena to St. Joseph and had received a response to my request, in this case, before I had even finished the nine days of prayer! With a big smile, she answered, "I'm not surprised. That's just how Joe rolls."

Given the profound responsibility St. Joseph had in caring for and providing for the Christ Child and the Mother of God, we can trust in his intercession to seek the best possible course of action on our behalf. Just as Joseph obediently followed the will of God and sought the best for Jesus and Mary, we can be confident that he will do no less for us.

St. Raphael

One of the seven archangels who stand before the throne of the Lord is St. Raphael, the patron saint of singles, bodily ills, and young people. You might remember him from the Old Testament book of Tobit. In the story, the archangel was sent by God to help Tobit, his son Tobiah, and Tobiah's wife-to-be, Sarah, whose seven previous husbands perished on their wedding nights. Not exactly what you call a desirable situation to marry into! But with the help of St. Raphael, Tobit's son was able to break the tragic trend and marry the beautiful Sarah without fear of death.

It was because of St. Raphael's instrumental help in bringing Tobiah and his beautiful wife together that the archangel is named the patron of singles. Like Tobit, Tobiah, and Sarah, we can also learn from Raphael to be courageous and have faith in God even in seemingly insurmountable situations. And who knows: if you are searching for your future husband or wife, St. Raphael just might be able to help you. After all, he's also the patron saint of happy meetings!

Saints for Singles

St. Catherine of Siena (1347–1380)

Although she lived more than six hundred years ago, St. Catherine of Siena is a fine role model for today's single women. Assertive and strong, yet humble and kind, Catherine spent much of her life working for the Church during a socially and politically contentious time in Europe. Born in 1347 as the twenty-fourth of twenty-five children, she experienced a vision of Christ at the tender age of six. While passing in front of Siena's San Domenico Church, she saw a vision of Jesus, who smiled at her, blessed her, and left her in a state of spiritual ecstasy. By the age of seven, she had taken a vow of chastity, revealing to her parents that she would never marry. After much consternation, her parents eventually relented, and while still in her teens, Catherine began wearing the traditional black and white habit as a member of the Third Order of Saint Dominic. While continuing to live at home, she led a life of solitude and near-complete silence in a small cell while serving as household servant to her parents and siblings. Later, her confessor and biographer, Father Raymond of Capua, wrote that during this time of "preparation," Catherine experienced a mystical marriage to Christ and was eventually told by Jesus to leave her withdrawn existence, mix with her fellow men, and learn to serve them.

Heeding our Lord's call, Catherine dedicated much of her life to helping Siena's poor and sick. During this time, she also began traveling throughout Italy with a band of earnest associates urging reform of the clergy and support for the crusades and settling disputes between republics, principalities, and powerful Italian families. But her preferred method of communication was writing letters; she corresponded with everyone from popes and royals to prisoners and peasants. Foremost among her letters was

Single and Catholic

her long correspondence with Pope Gregory XI. At her urging, the pope eventually heeded her advice and moved back to Rome, officially ending the Avignon Papacy in 1377. In 1970, Pope Paul VI gave St. Catherine the title of Doctor of the Church, making her one of the four female Doctors in Church history.

It is reported that while at prayer, Satan would assail Catherine with thoughts of sexual temptation. To combat this, she battled back by increasing her prayers and humility and remained confident in the helping hand of God. With perseverance, she was eventually able to overcome the temptations and today, along with other patronages, is the patron saint of those battling with sexual temptation.

What Catherine accomplished in her short life of just thirty-three years reminds us that we are all called to use our time wisely in serving our family, our Church, and people from all walks of life. St. Catherine maximized the graces and gifts she received and used them with gusto in the service of God and the salvation of souls.

As singles, we can learn much from this courageous and spirited saint, while seeking her intercession for the temptations we face in our own contentious times. St. Catherine calls us to have courage in the face of difficulty while having a tireless trust that God will see us through, no matter how great the challenges we face.

St. Augustine of Hippo (354–430)

You may be wondering why the patron saint of theologians and beer brewers is included in this chapter. Prior to his conversion, much of Saint Augustine's young adulthood was spent partying, carousing, and in pursuit of worldly pleasures. One of his most famous lines was this prayer: "Give me chastity and continence, but not yet."[14] After many years of living a life steeped in false beliefs and wild living, Augustine had a profound conversion and today serves as an inspiration to many who are battling with their own vices. After years of tearful prayers and intercession by his holy mother, St. Monica, and with the influence of their preacher friend, St. Ambrose, Augustine eventually turned from his pagan ways and embraced Christianity.

After his conversion, Augustine was baptized and went on to become a priest and later a bishop of Hippo as well as a Doctor of the Church and founder of a religious order of priests. The writings of this Christian theologian and philosopher influenced to a great extent the development of Western Christianity and Western philosophy. His most well-known works are *The Confessions* and *The City of God.*

"Too late have I loved You," Augustine once cried to God.[15] But with his decision and commitment to live a holy life, the repentant saint made up for the actions of his youth. From party boy to one of the greatest saints who ever lived, St. Augustine shows us that no matter what sins we may have committed, it is never too late to make a fresh start by committing ourselves to God. When we do, amazing things begin to happen!

St. Margaret of Cortona (1247–1297)

St. Margaret of Cortona is a patron saint for modern challenges. As a beautiful young woman, Margaret became the mistress of a young nobleman named Arsenio. Although Arsenio made it clear that he would never marry her, the two lived together for

---

[14] St. Augustine, *Confessions*, trans. Rex Warner (New York: Mentor Press, 1963), 174.
[15] Ibid., 235.

nearly a decade. During this time, they had a son. As time went by, Margaret hoped in vain that Arsenio would change his mind and become her husband. Although he eventually promised her that they would marry, that day never came. When Arsenio was found murdered, the event shook Margaret so deeply that it caused her to reevaluate her life and to begin to live differently. Placing God first in her life, Margaret eventually sought refuge with the Franciscan friars at Cortona. While there, she joined the Third Order of St. Francis and began working as a nurse to the elderly. She also saw her son became a friar.

Canonized in 1728, St. Margaret remains the patron of any-one — man or woman — who has turned away from a sinful life. She is also the patron of mothers who, for whatever reason, are raising their children alone. If you are a single mom, why not enlist the special intercession of St. Margaret, who understands the struggles and challenges that come with raising children as a single parent? Margaret is a strong example of how solace and redemption can be found in the Faith and that, with God, you never walk alone.

St. Helen (249–329)

As the mother of Constantine, St. Helen is most widely known as the finder of the True Cross in Jerusalem. That's why, for many centuries, devotion to St. Helen has been linked to devotion to the Holy Cross. But there is another facet to this remarkable woman that few know about. In A.D. 289, after twenty-two years of marriage, which produced their son Constantine, Helen's husband, the Roman Emperor Constantius, left her in order to marry a younger woman who was a member of Rome's imperial family.

But Helen did not let the end of her marriage define who she was. After her divorce, she converted to Christianity and became a devout servant of God. Beyond serving the poor and the destitute, she became an important figure in the Church for her pilgrimage to the Holy Land, where it is said she discovered the True Cross of Christ along with other holy relics from the Crucifixion.

As civil divorce and marital upheaval remain prevalent in today's society, St. Helen is a powerful example for unhappy spouses and those who are separated or divorced and a heavenly patron who can truly sympathize with their anguish and offer prayers on their behalf.

Our Guardian Angel

Beyond the saints listed above, we must not forget about the constant companion we have in our guardian angel, whom God has placed by our side. Appointed to us as guides and protectors throughout our lives, our guardian angels "always behold the face of [the] Father who is in heaven" (Matt. 18:10) and are with us from the beginning of our existence until we enter our eternal home. In Luke 4:10–11, we find the divine commission that God has given to each of our angels: "He will give his angels charge of you, to guard you," and "On their hands they will bear you up, lest you strike your foot against a stone."

Sadly, some of us go through life unaware that we have such a faithful friend by our side, while others barely acknowledge their devoted angel. But every now and then, we hear of stories in which someone credits his guardian angel for sparing his life or protecting him in a dangerous situation. Perhaps you have such a story. It's important to recognize that our angels are with us not only to defend us from evil but also to reprimand our conscience and pray with us and for us.

If you haven't prayed to your guardian angel in a while, think about taking some time each day to acknowledge his presence and thank him for his assistance and hidden protection. We would do well to honor this great companion God has placed at our side! A simple prayer that you might have learned as a child is a great way to do this.

> Angel of God, my guardian dear,
> to whom God's love commits me here,
> ever this day [or night] be at my side,
> to light and guard, to rule and guide. Amen.

These are just a few of the saints and angels who can inspire those who are unmarried, those who are civilly divorced, and those raising children on their own. There are thousands of holy men and woman who are recognized by the Catholic Church as saints. Let's face it—we can all use help in trying to live better lives. It is reassuring to know that the heavenly court is filled with angels and saints who not only inspire us but are eager to help us—if only we will call upon them. We must also remember that saints are made, not born. Like the saints, we are also called to work in cooperation with God's grace and mercy to grow holier in our daily lives. It is what the saints did—and it is what we are also called to do.

6

The Power of One:
Singles in the New Evangelization

When we hear the word *evangelization*, what might come to mind for some of us are images of modern-day megachurch pastors preaching in stadium-size venues or reaching celebrity status through televangelism. Others may think of Billy Graham, the highly respected and beloved American Christian evangelist and spiritual adviser to several U.S. presidents, whose revival meetings, more commonly known as "crusades," have impacted the lives of millions across the globe. Why is it, then, that when we hear the word applied to our own Faith, we are unclear as to how relevant it is to us? What can we single Catholics offer the Church in ways of evangelization?

What Is the New Evangelization?

In his 1975 apostolic exhortation *Evangelii Nuntiandi* (On Evangelization in the Modern World), Venerable Pope Paul VI pointed out the critical role of evangelization in the Church, saying, "Evangelizing is, in fact, the grace and vocation proper to the Church, her deepest identity. She [the Church] exists in order to evangelize."[16]

---

[16] Pope Paul VI, *Evangelii Nuntiandi*, December 8, 1975, no. 14.

In a more recent document by the United States Conference of
Catholic Bishops (USCCB) called "What Is Evangelization?" the
bishops define *evangelization* as "bringing the Good News of Jesus
into every human situation and seeking to convert individuals and
society by the divine power of the Gospel itself." The USCCB
further states that "at its essence — it is the proclamation of salvation in Jesus Christ and the response of a person in faith, which
are both works of the Spirit of God."[17]

One dictionary definition for the word *evangelize* is simply "to
share enthusiasm for specific beliefs and ideals." So what does
the term *New Evangelization*, thrown around in Catholic circles,
mean for us? During his pontificate, St. John Paul II emphasized
a fresh call to *all of the Christian faithful* to evangelize in the spirit
of the Second Vatican Council and in solidarity with the prior
call to evangelization by Pope Paul VI. John Paul II first used
the term *New Evangelization* in 1983 when he addressed the
Catholic bishops of Latin America in Haiti saying, "The com-
memoration of the half millennium of evangelization will gain
its full energy if it is a commitment, not to re-evangelize but to a
New Evangelization, new in its ardor, methods and expression."[18]
With this, St. John Paul II ushered in the call for *new* "methods
and expression" of evangelization that specifically ask each of
us to get enthusiastic about our Faith and share it joyfully with
others, just as the apostles did so long ago.

[17] "What Is Evangelization?— Go and Make Disciples," United
States Conference of Catholic Bishops, accessed May 11, 2015,
http://www.usccb.org/beliefs-and-teachings/how-we-teach/
evangelization/go-and-make-disciples/what_is_evangeliza-
tion_go_and_make_disciples.cfm.
[18] Pope John Paul II, address to CELAM, *L'Osservatore Romano*,
April 18, 1983, 9.

Singles in the New Evangelization

In the 1990 encyclical *Redemptoris Missio* (*Mission of the Redeemer*), St. John Paul II addressed three areas of focus of the New Evangelization: (1) preaching to those who have never heard the gospel, (2) preaching to those Christian communities where the Church is present and who have fervor in their faith, and (3) preaching to those Christian communities who have ancient roots but who "have lost a living sense of the faith, or even no longer consider themselves members of the Church, and live a life far removed from Christ and his Gospel."[19] In this case what is needed is a *new evangelization* or a *re-evangelization*.

Making the New Evangelization a pillar of his own pontificate, Pope Emeritus Benedict XVI established the Pontifical Council for the New Evangelization in 2010. In 2012, a synod was also held to discuss the New Evangelization further. In his postsynodal apostolic exhortation, Pope Benedict said:

> Our own time, then, must be increasingly marked by a new hearing of God's word and a new evangelization. Recovering the centrality of the divine word in the Christian life leads us to appreciate anew the deepest meaning of the forceful appeal of Pope John Paul II: to pursue the *missio ad gentes* [to the nations] and vigorously to embark upon the new evangelization, especially in those nations where the Gospel has been forgotten or meets with indifference as a result of widespread secularism.[20]

Singles Play a Crucial Role in the New Evangelization

As Catholic singles who are trying to live our Faith in a secular world, the last part of Pope Benedict's statement, "where the

---

[19] Pope John Paul II, *Redemptoris Missio*, December 7, 1990, no. 8.
[20] Pope Benedict XVI, *Verbum Domini*, no. 122.

Gospel has been forgotten or meets with indifference as a result of widespread secularism"[21] might resonate with many of us. Because of the secularization of the world, there is perhaps no more important time in history than the present moment to become engaged in evangelizing others. Whether it is taking the first necessary step of growing in our Faith so we can better evangelize others and live our Christian witness more effectively, or in our conviction in reaching out with the knowledge we have now to help encourage others in their faith journey—never underestimate the critical role you play in bringing the gospel message of Christ to others.

Catholic singles have been profoundly impacted by the secularization of the world. Therefore, we may recognize more than most people how the New Evangelization could also be described as a call to arms for the faithful to oppose secularization and seek out those who have succumbed to it. It is also a call to reach out to those who have slowly drifted away from the Church; those who no longer consider themselves members of the Church; or those who claim our Faith but live a life far removed from the truth Jesus gave us. I am unhappily confident that the majority of us have family members, relatives, or friends who were once baptized but no longer practice the Faith. Beyond those we know personally, it is not hard to see the need for evangelization all around us. Perhaps, to some degree we may recognize that we are also among those who have slowly drifted from our Faith and may be in need of support and encouragement to begin again.

---

[21] Pope Benedict XVI, *The Liturgy Documents: Supplemental Documents for Parish Worship, Devotions, Formation and Catechesis*, ed. Mark Wedig, Joyce Ann, and Corina Laughlin (Chicago: Liturgy Training Publications, 2013), 154.

Singles in the New Evangelization

The New Evangelization is an invitation to committed Catholics to meet today's tremendous need to reach out and share our Faith with others, particularly Catholics who may no longer practice the Faith. As such, singles have a wonderful opportunity to play a crucial role in the New Evangelization. This might sound dramatic, but that makes it no less real: all committed Catholics, no matter what their vocation or state in life, have a sacred duty to reach out to other souls.

Because of our perspective as singles and because we are out there on the front lines of the secular world, we have a unique opportunity to evangelize powerfully by example through living a lifestyle that is in keeping with our Faith. We have an opportunity, every single day, to reach out to those closest to us who might have fallen away, by sharing our enthusiasm for our beliefs; this, in turn, may touch their hearts and inspire them to remember that God loves them unconditionally and can change their lives too. All the enthusiasm in the world will get us nowhere if we do not seek the grace of God to guide us as we reach out to others. The New Evangelization calls all followers of Christ to be formed in the Faith. But it means that *we have to live it first.* We do this by going to Mass, receiving the sacrament of Reconciliation often, and staying in touch with God through prayer and through reading the Bible and other spiritual books. These practices help us open ourselves to Him so we may receive the grace necessary for God to guide us. God's way will always be the most effective way, so why not go with it?

Since evangelization is the essential mission of the Church, it makes sense that it should also be the central mission of our lives. When we know the goodness of God on a personal level, why would we not want that for other people? As Catholic singles, we've got a lot to bring to the table. We are each called to tap into our unique God-given talents and use them to respond however He leads us in drawing others to seek an awakening of their faith.

I am not talking only about preaching at people and pontificating. You can evangelize through a music ministry or by teaching catechism or Rite of Christian Initiation of Adults (RCIA) classes. If you have a passion for politics, you could evangelize by running for public office on a faithful platform. Or you could write or speak about your Faith or simply live out your Faith through your thoughts, words, and deeds—which is huge! All of us have talents that can be used to bring people closer to God, and we shouldn't hesitate to use them.

When you think about what the New Evangelization means for you, it is encouraging to consider that there are so many ways we can reach out to others. The Church is inviting each of us to ask God and ourselves, in a very personal way, how we can share in the New Evangelization through our lives. It is a critical call to action—a call that invites us to reach out to souls in a time of escalating secularism and moral relativism.

The New Evangelization is a call for everyone to become involved. We must not only develop our faith life and spirituality but must also reach out to others within the framework of our experience. Those who are divorced, separated, or widowed or are single parents can be especially influential in witnessing to others who are struggling with their faith during times of marriage difficulties, a failed marriage, the loss of a spouse, or the tremendous challenge of parenting alone.

Know Your Faith, Then Share It

We have a great responsibility when we evangelize—one that calls us to know our Faith and to be able to speak knowledgeably about it to others. Not all of us grew up in devout families or received a Catholic education. The Church is full of cradle Catholics who are amazed to discover the richness of the Faith that they were baptized in, once they really look at it. One of the most gratifying experiences we can have as "evangelists" is to watch the amazement of a fellow Catholic as he begins to discover anew the richness of our Faith. It is very important that we do what we can to know our Faith and to be active in it, so that we can live it more fully in our lives and effectively share it with others.

You don't have to have a degree in theological studies or apologetics to evangelize. Many wonderful resources are available to help us learn more about the Church and even about how to evangelize others. We can begin by becoming more familiar with the central teachings of our Faith through knowing and living the Ten Commandments and reading Holy Scripture and the *Catechism of the Catholic Church*. The USCCB's website has an entire section devoted to the New Evangelization, and individual dioceses and parishes have events and materials devoted to helping Catholics learn more about the Faith and understanding the vital role we can play by witnessing to others.

Part of the New Evangelization also includes being knowledgeable about Catholic moral teachings. As Catholic singles, we have clear moral obligations that influence all aspects of our lives, whether in the workplace, in the voting booth, in healthcare ethics, or in any of the myriad choices the world presents us with at each moment. We are at a pivotal point in our history where religious freedoms are under attack and Christians are being persecuted and martyred for their most deeply held beliefs.

One example that surprised me was to hear that during Super Bowl XLIX in Phoenix, a visiting Bible-based church picketed

outside a Catholic church in protest against our "worship" of
Mary. These small attacks as well as the increasing deadly violence against Christians throughout our world emphasize just
how imperative it is that we know how to engage in defending
our Faith among those who wish to chip away at or misrepresent
our moral teachings. That is why every Catholic should be edu-
cated in the five Catholic nonnegotiables (see below); we have
a moral obligation not only to know them but also to educate
others about them. It is also imperative that we are guided by
them at the voting booth so that we do not support candidates
or legislation inconsistent with Catholic moral teaching. There
are great online resources available for learning more about these
five nonnegotiable moral principles:

- Abortion
- Euthanasia
- Embryonic stem-cell research
- Human cloning
- Same-sex marriage

Obviously, these are *hot* issues. We might be challenged in our
beliefs and compelled to speak out in defense of moral truth.
Education and preparation will enable you to share your Faith
fearlessly, while compassionately meeting other people where
they are in their faith formation.

We Catholics who are in the single state can make the best
use of our time by learning our Faith, finding the best way to
defend the Church's moral teachings, and approaching those
around us with a love that desires to see them embrace Christ
and His Church. As we said above, making good use of our
time is the best way to spend our single lives so that we can

become the defenders and evangelizers that the Church needs right now.

In Defense of Life

Nowhere in these days is evangelization more profoundly needed than in defense of human life from the moment of conception until natural death. At this time, the United States has marked more than forty years since the *Roe v. Wade* decision that legalized abortion in all fifty states at virtually any time during pregnancy, for any reason. If you run the math, the number of abortions in the United States is downright shocking. Every day since *Roe*, on average, 3,767 babies are killed by abortion; that works out to 157 unborn babied killed every hour of every day across America.[22] As single Catholics, we can play a major role in actively contributing to the renewal of society articulating Catholic teachings on the dignity of human life. Our voice is particularly important in the pro-life movement because it is overwhelmingly assumed in the mainstream media and among left-wing political groups that if you are single and especially if you are a female, you must be pro-choice.

Therefore, it is essential for single men and single women who are Catholic to stand up for the sanctity of life. As our culture becomes predominantly abortion centered, we continue to witness an insidious reprogramming of the public against the value of individual life while conversely exalting the value of individual choice. Therefore, we must develop the skills necessary

---

[22] Steven Ertelt, "57,762,169 Abortions in America Since Roe vs. Wade in 1973," LifeNews.com, January 21, 2015, accessed July 17, 2015, http://www.lifenews.com/2015/01/21/57762169-abortions-in-america-since-roe-vs-wade-in-1973/.

to articulate the Church's teachings on the value and dignity of each human person.

It is also vital to recognize that we live in a time that typifies what is meant by the statement: "The only thing necessary for the triumph of evil is for good men to do nothing."[23] The assault against the sanctity of women as life givers is waged when whole countries fail to protect, and in fact legally condone, the termination of unplanned pregnancies while the abortion industry makes billions from the exploitation of women in crisis. Tragically, today's culture of death does not uphold a women's unique ability to conceive and bear a child but instead considers the unborn child an inconvenience or justifiably disposable if the child is not of a desirable gender or is deemed physically imperfect. Therefore, Pope Francis calls each of us to engage in pro-life activities with vigor, saying, "Defend the unborn against abortion even if they persecute you, calumniate you, set traps for you, take you to court or kill you."[24]

In what ways might God be calling you to witness to and work to help ensure the inherent value and dignity of human life?

Share Your Story

There is nothing more powerful than sharing your personal conversion story or stories from your past in order to witness to the saving power of Jesus Christ in your life. By sharing how God

---

[23] Edmund Burke, *The Intellectual Life of Edmund Burke*, ed. David Bromwich (Cambridge: Belknap Press, 2014), 176.

[24] Eric Scheidler, "Pope Francis: Defend the Unborn from Abortion Even if Persecuted," LifeNews.com, March 14, 2013, accessed July 17, 2015, http://www.lifenews.com/2013/03/14/pope-francis-defend-the-unborn-from-abortion-even-if-persecuted/.

has touched your life and how practicing your Faith has enriched your life, you can inspire others to want to return to the Church or to take their faith life more seriously.

Whether you are a cradle Catholic or have recently completed RCIA and entered the Church, you have your own story of how Christ has worked miracles in your life or how you've relied on your faith when things got tough. By sharing your story with others, you are coming from a place of experience and authenticity; so never underestimate how sharing your encounters with the living God can affect the life of another!

Witnessing through Social Media

It's hard to escape social media! There will be 179.7 million people across the United States who will spend time on social media. Facebook leads the way with 156.5 million estimated users, followed by Instagram, with 60.3 million users, and Twitter, with 52.9 million users. I mention this because, like it or not, social media has become a central means of communications for many, and it's not just for the young. In 2016, Facebook will experience the largest percentage-share increase ever in the 65-and-over age demographic.[25] And while social media can bring out the worst in people, including downright nasty comments and bullying, it can also be an outstanding tool to evangelize and engage others positively in faith-based conversation and healthy debate. According to Archbishop Claudio Celli, head of the Pontifical Council for Social Communications, "Unless the Church engages social media, we will wind up talking to ourselves." He

---

[25] Kristin Piombino, "Infographic: The Social Networks People Will Use in 2015," Ragan.com, January 26, 2015, accessed July 17, 2105, http://www.ragan.com/Main/Articles/49236.aspx.

also goes on to say, "Our presence [in digital media] will only be effective if we are authentic witnesses to our faith."[26] The Vatican certainly understands this, and in 2012 Pope Benedict sent his first personal tweet to the world. Just one hour after his first tweet, the pontiff had seven hundred thousand followers on his English-language account alone! Pope Francis also knows the value of communicating through social media and has millions of Twitter followers across the globe. Clearly, social media is a powerful way to communicate!

There is also no shortage of Catholic organizations, bishops, priests, and religious with their own Facebook pages and Twitter accounts who use these tools to communicate messages designed to inspire, inform, and draw us closer to God. As Catholic singles, we too can leverage our social-media knowledge to reach out to others by sharing positive, consoling, and faith-filled messages that bring the Good News of Christ and His Church into the digital landscape that has become new mission territory for the Church.

Witnessing through Our Everyday Actions

We can be witnesses to our Faith through our everyday actions by bringing our Faith into all aspects of our lives. This can include simple acts of kindness, such as offering an encouraging word to another, listening to those who simply need to be heard, and showing care and respect to those around us, even those who aren't so easy to get along with. We can witness indirectly by

[26] David Gibson, "Vatican Media Chief Says the Church Can't Ignore Social Media," Religious News Service, May 23, 2014, accessed July 17, 2015, http://www.religionnews.com/2014/05/23/vatican-media-chief-says-church-cant-ignore-social-media/.

saying Grace at mealtimes, remaining silent in the face of off-color humor, and avoiding gossip.

In this society that downplays good manners, men can speak volumes by performing simple acts of chivalry, such holding doors for women and generally treating them with respect. Women have a standard to live up to as well as witness to the virtue of modesty in the way we dress, carry, and conduct ourselves, while still remaining stylish! In a world where so little is left to the imagination, modesty shows others that we have more important things to offer than just our bodies.

We must never underestimate the powerful witness we also have in performing public acts of faith such as going to church each Sunday, partaking in the sacraments of Holy Communion and Reconciliation, spending a Holy Hour in Eucharistic Adoration, observing holy days of obligation, receiving ashes on Ash Wednesday, and observing Sunday as a holy day of rest in this world filled with nonstop activity. We never know how such simple acts of faith might affect those around us, including close family members who might not be practicing any faith at all.

The New Evangelization is a powerful missionary moment to which we are all called. We don't have to be perfect to have an important role in bringing Christ to others—all we need is a willingness to do God's will and to be "His hands and His feet" in our spiritually thirsty world. The New Evangelization is a clarion call to each of us, no matter what our state or vocation, to discover what our role can be and to be generous in our response. As we labor in the virtues of love, humility, faith, charity, and mercy, through God's grace, we have all the essential tools we need to be effective missionaries in the modern world. Through living the virtues, we are directed to be patient and not push; to be merciful and nonjudgmental and to listen more than we talk.

Because we are sinners, we might feel we are not worthy to engage in evangelizing others. Or maybe we feel as if we take two steps forward and one step back in our spiritual lives and therefore we have no right to speak to others about Jesus or Church teachings. Yet Pope Francis calls us to have confidence in evangelizing anyway: "If you make a mistake, you get up and go forward; that is the way. Those who do not walk in order not to err make the more serious mistake." So all you really need to do is say yes and be willing to begin. From there God will show you where to go and what to do as He takes your yes and builds upon it.

Finally, the New Evangelization is meant to bring about an authentic renewal of the Church so that she can undertake a new missionary outreach to the whole world. As part of the one, holy, catholic, and apostolic Church founded by Jesus Christ and guided by the Holy Spirit, and sent by the Holy Trinity into the world, Catholic singles can play an integral role in bringing the world into communion with God and His Church. While you might struggle to find your place in the Church as a single person, you are called to bear witness to the world, and that can be even more remarkable as a single person who brings a unique perspective to the world. It may be the power of one to take the loving and healing words of Christ to a world that is so hungry for it.

Each and every committed heart holds the possibility of changing the world through the New Evangelization. Take up the challenge and find out for yourself—the Power of One!

7

The Narrow Way — Why It's Worth It!

Filmed entirely on location in Spain and France, *The Way* (2010), tells the story of Tom Avery, who decides to walk the ancient pilgrimage along the Camino de Santiago, or the Way of Saint James, as a memorial to his recently deceased son. It is often reflected how similar our life is to a pilgrimage, walking along a rocky path and praying with each step, and this film is often a reflection of that as it follows a grieving father who traces the famous path on which countless pilgrims have trudged.

Although the film does not delve much into the psyche of Tom, we sense that he is fighting a battle for greater meaning in life. The film ends with beautiful interior footage of the pilgrimage's termination, the Cathedral of Santiago de Compostela, which houses the remains of St. James the Apostle. It is implied that, having completed the journey, Tom has returned to the Catholic Faith and found peace.

This film presents a powerful visual metaphor of our own path in life — our own Camino de Santiago. Much like the journey of the film's central character, our journey as singles can be filled with many twists and turns. There are times when our way may be smooth and joyful. It may be filled with adventure, family, friends, success, and a strong faith life. At other times, we may hit rocky patches — perhaps experiencing the pain of a broken relationship, financial hardships, job loss, health problems, spiritual dryness, or a general fear of what might be around the next curve in the road.

There is certainly no shortage of things that can lead us off our path into much rockier terrain. Fleshly pleasures and unsavory enticements of all kinds — some even a few keystrokes away on our computers — are available to us 24-7. We live in a culture obsessed with the secular, including self-indulgences of all kinds, the accumulation of status symbols, and all-time-high rates of consumerism, despite record-breaking consumer debt!

Yet Jesus reaches out amid the frenzied pace, noise, and distractions of our times to invite all of us to follow Him on a different road — a road that He Himself walked well before us with bruised and bloodied feet. Sadly, many in the world today don't see much value in taking His road. It's an unpopular route. Even Jesus does not promise it will be easy — but only that in the end, it will be worth it.

> Enter by the narrow gate; for the gate is wide and the way is easy, that leads to destruction, and those who enter by it are many. For the gate is narrow and the way is hard, that leads to life, and those who find it are few. (Matt. 7:13–14)

Jesus tells us not only to enter through the narrow gate and travel the constricted road but also to pick up our cross in our single state and follow Him, and not just every once in a while or only when we feel like it, but *daily* — meaning always and everywhere. In fact, it is a requirement for gaining heaven!

> If any man would come after me, let him deny himself and take up his cross daily and follow me. For whoever

would save his life will lose it; and whoever loses his life for my sake, he will save it. For what does it profit a man if he gains the whole world and loses or forfeits himself? (Luke 9:23–25)

And so it is wise to reflect and ask ourselves, "What road am I on?"

Getting Back on the Road

Although today he is a devout Marian Priest, Father Donald Calloway, MIC, is a powerful example of how the mercy of God can work directly in our lives and how He can lead us back on the right path, if we let Him. In his book *No Turning Back: A Witness to Mercy*, Father Calloway retells the dramatic story of his adolescent years, when heroin, cocaine, marijuana, and LSD were his drugs of choice—and that was before he turned eighteen! After spending his teen years abusing drugs and being arrested several times, his life took a miraculous turn one night while he lived with his parents.

Feeling empty and hating his life, he found a book on our Lady, Queen of Peace, which led to his conversion and ardent love of Mary and the Church. With an increased desire to learn more about Jesus, our Lady, and the Faith, Calloway decided to become a Catholic.

Father Calloway's story shows us just what can happen when we exit the wide road and allow ourselves to be transformed by the saving power of Jesus Christ. In our conversation, Father Calloway emphasized, "Our God is a very merciful Father." Father Calloway assures each of us that the sacrament of Confession is available and we can go "an endless number of times." Father also notes, "We need to trust in the endless mercy and goodness of Jesus and have total confidence in Him. We are weak, but His mercy is greater than our weakness."

As we've seen, there are many distractions in this world, and many of them can pull us off the narrow way that leads to mercy and peace. Although all of us struggle, single Catholics often find that the burden seems to be a lonely one full of many trials and errors. Some might not even be sinful, at least in appearance. We might focus too much on our careers or personal aspirations, at the cost of our prayer life. Perhaps we turn to those because God doesn't seem to be giving us the answer we want. We may not have lived the crazy life that Father Calloway lived in his youth, but we can find the same mercy of Jesus that will put us on the right path and continue to offer us direction, no matter how lost and distracted we get.

Food for the Journey

We can't travel the narrow road without sustenance, however. We need fuel for the often difficult journey of daily life. As Catholics, we receive strength for the journey by receiving our Lord Jesus Christ, true God and true man, fully present in the Eucharist. The Holy Eucharist not only strengthens us as we walk the narrow road mapped out for us by Christ but also gives us the graces needed to separate ourselves from sin and to rid ourselves of all distraction. "The body of Christ we receive in Holy Communion is 'given up for us,' and the blood we drink 'shed for many for the forgiveness of sins.' For this reason the Eucharist cannot unite us to Christ without at the same time cleansing us from past sins and preserving us from future sins" (CCC 1393).

As someone who has traveled both roads, Father Calloway says the narrow road is worth everything. Sure, it's the way that demands more, challenges more, and begs us to seek more, but

The Narrow Way — Why It's Worth It!

it is also a path that fulfills us in a way that the world never can. It leads us not to a dead end but to a world without end. "It not only leads to eternal life with Jesus, but it's also because we are made for greatness," explains Father Calloway. "If we aren't striving for sanctity and virtue and holiness, we are basically a bunch of monkeys throwing rocks around. Society tells us we are going nowhere. Yet we know we are made by a loving Creator who wants us to enter into a relationship with Him for all eternity. If this requires walking the narrow path in life, then let's get going!"

Father Calloway urges us to cultivate a close relationship with God, just as we would with those we care most about. "It's important to remember that we are in a relationship with God," says Father Calloway. "As in any committed relationship, including marriage, it requires perseverance. This means that you are faithful to Him in good times and in bad, in sickness and in health, for better and for worse."

The world wants us to think that by taking the narrow road, we have embarked on a pointless journey and committed ourselves to a boring, meaningless path. But this is not the case! When we commit to walking in the footsteps of Christ, we receive an abundance of joy, peace, and love that all the treasures of the world could never fulfill. Sure, we will continue to have our ups and downs, but we will also have the strength and power of God on our side to help us through it all. God also assures us that He has specific plans for our good:

> For I know the plans I have for you, says the LORD, plans for welfare and not for evil, to give you a future and a hope. (Jer. 29:11)

Going back to *The Way*, we are often thrown on roads that are strange and sometimes a little frightening. Through this path, though, God makes us into what we are truly meant to be. We have a destination, which we know is life with Jesus, but our path will take us through many places and points along the way. Instead of seeing your single life as temporary period, think of it as part of pilgrimage. You are not a single person waiting for what comes next; you are following after Christ on the narrow way and are becoming greater than you could have ever imagined.

The best part of seeing our life as a pilgrimage is that we don't have to know the full details of what we'll encounter. We just need to know where we want to be and to start walking!

A common attitude among singles today is to put the "spiritual stuff" off until later in life and just focus on having a good time now. Yet, as Catholic singles, we need to pay particular attention to how we are spending the precious time that God has given us *now* for our journey. Jesus makes it clear that He is "the way, and the truth, and the life; no one comes to the Father, but by me" (John 14:6). Therefore, we must do our best to live faithfully in the present moment by following in Christ's footsteps and trusting in His loving plans for our lives.

The world or the Way—which path will you choose?

8

Soul Searching: Discovering God's Will for Your Life

The word *strategic* is one we likely hear on a daily basis these days. In fact, it is one of the most overused buzzwords out there. In news broadcasts, for instance, we hear about global *strategic* initiatives, and in corporate boardrooms we hear about *strategic* plans. In our working lives we might also take part in strategic planning sessions about strategic staff initiatives, strategic growth assessments, strategic forecasting, strategic communications, et cetera—all of which require us to use strategic thinking!

Obviously, it is all about having a plan.

The *Oxford Dictionary* defines *strategic* as "relating to the identification of long-term or overall aims and interests and the means of achieving them." As important as it is to employ strategic planning in decision making, as most people would agree, how seriously do we apply the Oxford definition in our lives? It is easy to let the days pass by without really thinking about what our personal "strategic" plan is, what our long-term goals are, or how we want to spend our precious time on earth.

As spiritual beings and especially as Catholics, we believe that God has a plan for our lives. So the good news is that God has already done all the strategic planning for us! It is up to us, however, to discern and follow that plan. Unfortunately, it is also very easy to get caught up in the many distractions, distortions, and pleasures of today, which can make it difficult to pay attention to what God's will is for our lives. That means that discerning this plan is crucial for us who live in this world, so that we keep our focus solely on God and His plans for us. Since God has made each of us, He also speaks to each of us uniquely, through leadings and promptings of the Holy Spirit. Only in this way are we able to live in cooperation with Him and fulfill His plan for us based on our individuality, natural interests, gifts, talents, and inclinations.

What do you think God is calling you to do? Do you believe there is a plan, and how are you seeking to know it?

Since a vocation is a calling from God, it is up to us to be open to what God may be leading us to. However, no matter what vocation we are called to—married, single, priest, or religious—as Catholics we are all called to seek holiness through "loving the Lord our God with all our heart, and will all our soul, and with all our strength, and with all our mind, and our neighbor as ourselves" (cf. Luke 10:27). "It is in the Church," the *Catechism* states, "in communion with all the baptized, that the Christian fulfills his vocation," (CCC 2030). While all of us are called to this general vocation, God also has a plan for each of us and has given us a path. To begin discerning God's plan, we should first make sure we are participating in the life of the Church and then begin praying for God to reveal His particular path.

Nonetheless, there are times when it is hard to believe there is a plan, especially when the strategy we might have had in mind is not working for us. So how *do* we find our personal vocation, whatever it is?

Discovering God's Will for Your Life

Some individuals have been blessed to know very early in life what their vocation is. For others, it is not so clear. In time, through making *their* strategy to discern *God's* strategy, they found their way and in both instances.

Tales of Discernment

Have you ever met those people who seemed to have always known God's plan for them and then went after it without hesitation? In a perfect world, we would all know our vocation from an early age and then begin to pursue it. However, as many of us know, it isn't always that clear or that simple. Often our vocation is revealed to us a bit later in life.

The best way to begin discerning our path is to find those who have done a great deal of trying to understand God's plan for them and who have made great progress along the way. While I was trying to find some answers to how one begins to discern, I met some fantastic, faithful Catholics who offered priceless advice on discerning the plan God had for them.

Even among our bishops and clergy, finding and following God's plan can look quite different. The Most Rev. Bishop Thomas J. Olmsted, the Bishop of Phoenix, felt very early on that he knew that God's plan for him was to be a priest. So Bishop Olmsted found himself enrolling in seminary soon after high school and was ordained a priest in 1973 while still in his twenties. Meanwhile, the Most Rev. Robert D. Gruss, the Bishop of Rapid City, South Dakota, initially rejected a call to the priesthood but eventually discerned God's plan and was finally ordained a priest at the age of thirty-nine. Although both bishops discovered their vocation in different ways, their advice for us single Catholics is similar and helpful while we try to find our own path.

Single and Catholic

When it comes to starting out, both bishops strongly recommend prayer. "My advice for those discerning their vocation," Bishop Gruss told me, "is to keep praying—keep asking God, 'What is your will for my life?'" Bishop Olmsted echoes that advice when he states, "Obviously you have to have a life of prayer because a vocation is a call from God." While prayer may seem like an obvious step, one that many of us are already engaged in, it's an important one for finding our right path forward. More than that, when we pray, let's ask God what it is He wants us to do and be ready for the answer.

Father David Konderla, who spent four years as a vocations director before becoming the pastor and director of campus ministry of Saint Mary's Catholic Center at Texas A&M University, also stresses prayer for those who are starting to discern. In particular, Fr. Konderla recommends that we ask try to answer these questions while praying:

- What do I love?
- What is the source of my passion in life?
- What gifts and aptitudes and skills do I have?
- What do people whom I know well and who love me see in me?
- What do I want to grow old doing; what do I want my life to have meant?

As we ask these questions of us and of God, we will need to have discussions with others, and Fr. Konderla recommends possibly seeking out a spiritual director. A spiritual director is someone who gets to know you as a person and helps you to grow in holiness in your daily life. They can offer you guidance about prayer, service, and also help you to sort out your thoughts about what God might be calling you to. Bishop Olmsted agrees that a spiritual director is very important when discerning your future and your vocation, no matter what we might be called to it. If you're not sure where to start looking, Bishop Olsted offers this advice:

> A good way to do this is through making an annual retreat. If there is a good spiritual director or vocation director available at the retreat house, ask to have a chance to sit down with him. Share with him your thoughts on a vocation you are thinking about.

You can also look up monasteries or religious orders near you to see if they might offer spiritual direction. Some, like Opus Dei and the Benedictines, often make offering spiritual direction a part of their charism. And don't forget your own parish! Although many are afraid of bothering their priest, he might be a great source for you to find that spiritual direction while you move on to the next step. Your parish probably already advertises spiritual retreats, which you should take part in.

What kind of signs will you get that a particular vocation is right for you? Each person I talked to noted that discerning this means learning about yourself and focusing on finding God's will in your life. We each have individual talents that can be used for His greater glory, and it's important that we remain open to how to use them. While we pray and consider, we can keep a journal, be mindful of our reading habits, and really consider what it is we feel most at peace in doing with our time. "While others may see gifts and sense a call in us," cautions Fr. Paul Sullivan, another vocations director I spoke with, "ultimately the knowing of one's vocation comes from the interior sense of being at peace with a particular path." Fr. Sullivan notes that there will be times that we say, "Yes, that fits me," or "I am most myself when I'm on this path," but every path will still have its ruts and every vocation will certainly have its challenges. We should be able to face those challenges and still have a sense of peace, more importantly when we're at the end of our life and offer to God our vocational work.

As you consider and contemplate God's will, remember that you have one vocation that everyone is called to. In our discussions, Bishop Gruss stated it quite succinctly, "Our first and foremost vocation is seeking and doing the will of God, as baptized Catholic disciples." Paradoxically, when we remember this vocation that we all share, our particular vocation can often reveal itself over time. "Friendship with the Lord is the main vocation," as Fr. Konderla told me, and that friendship that we develop is how we get insight into our vocation. This friendship with the Lord we're all called to is about giving our love to the One who loved us first in all our prayer and praises. If we can live our life this way, always growing in our friendship with God, "it does not seem possible to miss the vocation." Fr. Michael Lightner, a priest in the Diocese of Milwaukee, agrees: "When we focus on God and give Him room to work in our lives and even take steps toward what we feel He's calling us to, amazing things will happen!"

No matter what path you might be called to, it's important that you act. Don't fall into a trap of constantly discerning or, as Bishop Olmsted said, daydreaming about a vocation. If you feel called to a religious vocation, it's important to start taking steps to follow through. That's also true with marriage, a career, or any path God might be calling you to. "One thing Satan loves," as Fr. Lightner told me, "is inaction." Sometimes, the action we need to undertake is simply to seek out someone who is living as we'd like to live and to learn from him what steps are needed.

This is why, as we saw earlier, prayer and spiritual direction can be invaluable as you continue to walk your path.

So what about those of us who are single and still hoping to marry, but are growing older and also growing impatient when it comes to finding a lack of eligible practicing Catholics out there? Along with working overtime on the virtue of patience, it's important to know that God's plans are still being revealed to us on a day-to-day basis, "for we have no idea what our life will be like tomorrow" (James 4:14). In the meantime, it's important to recognize that living life in the single state is not a wasted life, even if one should never marry or become a priest or a religious. Bishop Olmsted offers this advice:

> I think singles need to do all they can to grow in gratitude and joy from being a beloved son and beloved daughter of God. As we do that, it helps us to trust the Father who speaks to us as a loving Father and He will make our life fruitful.

Rather than think of your current single life as a waiting period or, worse, as a waste, consider that this is the time to grow in prayer and love. Doing this now will make you a better wife, husband, priest, or religious. The fact remains that we are to start our universal path, the one of holiness, *right now* while we might still have to figure out which unique plan God has for us. However, the many great folks that I talked to found that traveling this path and learning their plan was worth it, no matter how long they might have waited.

Pope Francis offers these words of encouragement:

> We need not be afraid; God follows the world of His hands with passion and skill in every phase of life. He never

abandons us! He has the fulfillment of His plan for us at heart, and yet He wishes to achieve it with our consent and cooperation.[27]

While you discern, my fellow single Catholics, we should have no fear about the path God has for us. It might be revealed to us tomorrow or years from now, but His plan is ultimately to bring us closer to Him in everlasting peace. This may not satisfy the world's idea of finding the perfect job and the perfect life, but it will bring us a greater sense of peace and the confidence to take on whatever comes up in our path.

[27] "Pope Francis' Message for 51st World Day of Prayer for Vocations," Zenit, January 16, 2014, accessed March 13, 2014, http://www.zenit.org/en/articles/pope-francis-message-for-51st-world-day-of-prayer-for-vocations.

9

Sleeping Single in a Double Bed— Why Chastity Matters

Saving yourself for marriage is often seen as old-fashioned, prud-ish, and out of touch with the times. Yet decades ago, remaining chaste prior to marriage was viewed as something to be prized, honored, and lauded by men and women alike. Following the teachings of St. Paul, chastity in early Christianity was promoted in order that one might emulate Christ and the Virgin Mary, and thus, virgins were thought to have had a special connection to God. Cherished and honored, they were described as a "jewel, a treasure, a sacred vessel, a temple of God."[28]

But nowadays, living with the collateral damage of the "sex-ual revolution," it is presumed by many that if you are an adult and actively dating, you are also sleeping with your partner. This is not surprising, considering that we live in a culture in which God's laws and even belief in God's existence are becoming in-creasingly "irrelevant" in the face of so many seeking to embrace

[28] Jane Tibbetts Schulenburg, *Forgetful of Their Sex: Female Sanc-tity and Society, ca. 500-1100* (Chicago: University of Chicago Press, 2001), 128.

humanistic moral codes. We singles especially have a calling to wrestle with this.

A key question we might ask ourselves is: "Am I contributing to a world in which human dignity is often disregarded in favor of personal convenience and self-serving gratification while dismissing the value and welfare of others?" After all, chastity is about respect for oneself and respect for others. This is why the Church teaches that to live unchastely in any way, even within a marriage, is an aberration from all that our sexuality is meant to be. If you are using your sexuality to focus on the pursuit of pleasure for pleasure's sake and for your own gratification without sincere love, consideration, and commitment to your partner, you are objectifying and dehumanizing yourself and the one you are with.

When you contemplate that the sexual act is so powerful that another human life and soul can be created as a result, it should be evident that there is far more to consider than "our physical needs." Our sexuality is a part of being human that requires us to be *wholly* human and to temper our sensuality with God's grace. This is why contraception is in direct opposition to the teachings of the Catholic Church and why it remains a hotly debated issue among the flock. It is a debate that the Church appears to be losing, since approximately 80 percent of Catholics are in favor of birth control. On July 25, 1968, Pope Paul VI issued his now famous encyclical letter *Humanae Vitae* (*Of Human Life*), which denounces all artificial forms of birth control as morally wrong. In favoring contraception and the world it brought, our culture fails to realize that the Church's intention is not to denounce our humanity but rather to emphasize the sacredness of our humanity and call us to honor ourselves and others as children of God. In the light of the Church, our sexuality is prized and should not be used for the mere satisfaction of pleasure.

Another consequence of our permissive sexual culture is abortion. National Right to Life, the nation's oldest and largest pro-life organization, believes that more than 56 million abortions have taken place in the United States since the Supreme Court's 1973 *Roe v. Wade* decision. By making it a legal right to be able to end the life of a child, *Roe v. Wade* has led not only to the deaths of tens of millions of innocent babies but also to untold sufferings for many of those now living with the emotional pain and consequences of having had an abortion. The current abortion numbers are staggering and indicative of what happens in a society that has abandoned the existence or relevancy of God's laws. Tragically, this has led us to a time when ultimately the sanctity of life itself is of little value.

Writing about the connection between the widespread use of contraceptives, abortion ,and nonmarital sex, Janet Smith, professor of moral theology at the Sacred Heart Major Seminary in Detroit, states:

> Most abortions are the result of unwanted pregnancies, most unwanted pregnancies are the result of sexual relationships outside marriage and most sexual relationships outside of marriage are facilitated by the availability of contraception. To turn the "progression" around: contraception leads to an increase in non-marital sex; an increase in non-marital sex leads to more unwanted pregnancies; more unwanted pregnancies lead to more abortions.[29]

[29] Reverend Walter J. Schu, L.C., "Contraception and Abortion: The Underlying Link," United States Conference of Catholic Bishops (USCCB) website, accessed July 15, 2015, http://www.usccb.org/issues-and-action/human-life-and-dignity/

Many young women are also increasingly finding themselves on their own in the difficult role of parenting as out-of-wedlock births continue to rise. According to the CDC, the percentage of births to unmarried women stands at 40.6 percent as of 2013.[30] These statistics indicate consequences that will impact everyone.

The downward spiral continues as we have reason to be greatly concerned about the power of the media and how our oversaturated TV and Internet culture sends a message of normalcy about open sexuality to both adults and minors. Whether it is through the "sex sells" tactics of advertisers, music videos, motion pictures, cable television, or prime-time programming, advertisers and entertainment companies continue to push the envelope with messages that are so contrary to Christian morality and Church teachings that it is frightening. Even more disturbing is that it is all based on the assumption that this is what Americans want in the way of entertainment.

Cable television and computers have also provided an opportunity to access pornographic material privately, and this has led to an escalating, pervasive, and serious increase in pornography addiction. According to a 2014 survey conducted by Proven Men Ministries, 64 percent of men view porn at least monthly, with the percentage of Christian men viewing at nearly the same rate.[31] And it is not just men. Increasing numbers of women are

---

contraception/articles-and-publications/contraception-and-abortion-the-underlying-link.cfm.

[30] Centers for Disease Control, "Unmarried Childbearing," accessed July 15, 2015, http://www.cdc.gov/nchs/fastats/unmarried-childbearing.htm.

[31] "Pornography Use and Addiction," ProvenMen, accessed May 11, 2015, http://www.provenmen.org/2014pornsurvey/pornography-use-and-addiction/.

also getting hooked on porn. The same survey cites that four in ten women (42 percent) between the ages of eighteen and thirty now view porn habitually.[32] Additional statistics provided by CovenantEyes.com, an Internet accountability and filtering website, show that the porn industry is now generating profits upwards of $13 billion annually in the United States.[33]

So, What Can We Do?

These statistics can seem overwhelming. Catholic singles who choose to follow God's moral laws are now in the minority. We have become the remnant—struggling to live the truth in a culture that tells us that premarital sexuality is just fine through a casual hookup with someone we might not even know well enough to lend our car to. Our culture gives legitimacy to lust at the cost of denigrating love and commitment. Is it any wonder that in today's society, those who choose to remain chaste before tying the knot are considered naive, undatable, sexually repressed, or just plain ridiculous?

Looking at the consequences of our culture, we stand as lights shining in the darkness when we choose chastity. Some of us have seen that when we buy into the lie that sex outside of marriage brings fulfillment, we buy into a distorted form of love that can lead us to depersonalize and discard others as objects for our own physical pleasure. That is why Christ's teachings clearly lead us to do all we can to work against today's skewed notions of sex, so that in purity of heart, our individual dignity can be restored

[32] Ibid.
[33] Sam Spencer, "How Big Is the Pornography Industry in the United States?," Covenant Eyes, June 1, 2012, accessed May 11, 2015, http://www.covenanteyes.com/2012/06/01/how-big-is-the-pornography-industry-in-the-united-states/.

and reset. Only in this way can we have a deeper understanding of the true "one flesh" union that is designed for marriage.

While sex outside of marriage is promoted widely as natural and even healthy, what is lost in the translation are the lasting wounds and disappointment we can experience when we've engaged in a sexual relationship without a lasting commitment. Why? Because it is the most intimate thing we as humans can ever experience and because God has willed that it exist within the exclusive context for which it was designed. God created marriage with the twofold purpose of bringing a married man and woman closer together in physical unity where they can freely express their love for one another and can take part in the creation of human life by being open to and welcoming children. When we give the deepest gift of ourselves away to others outside of this level of commitment, we are acting outside of God's design for human sexuality—a design whose purpose is to enhance life, not to cause harm to us and others; Church teaching contends that such harm is unavoidable when sexuality is used in any other way.

When we sleep with someone prior to marriage, we buy into the falsehood that love does not require concrete commitment. We may also feel that sex outside of marriage somehow makes us whole; that by having sex, we are now living a "normal" existence and that we are finally with the times. We may also buy into the false notion that our sexual bond will strengthen our relationship. Or we may simply yield to societal pressure, feeling that no option exists other than to have premarital sex if we ever hope to date and eventually marry. To be socially "acceptable," we are pressured to believe that sex is somehow an adult rite of passage and that it is expected that you must be in some kind of sexual relationship in order to be considered an authentic adult. Rarely revealed, however, is the deep level of confusion, anxiety, depression, emptiness, and even loneliness we can feel after giving our hearts and bodies to someone, only to find that deep down inside something is very wrong. How can it be otherwise, if there is no true commitment when engaging in the most profound act of trust with another?

Television shows, magazines, music videos, and even the growing popularity of erotic literature such as *Fifty Shades of Grey* try their best to glamorize sex or, in the case of *Fifty Shades*, even stylize sexual violence and gear it toward young women. What many fail to recognize, however, is that Hollywood's version of love is actually just lust in its many forms and not the committed, sacramental love that is the real deal. I speak of the type of marital love that lasts a lifetime and that builds families—the type of love that doesn't end with the empty promise of "I'll call you" and the heartbreak that follows when that promise isn't kept.

Even when we've made the choice to live chastely, though, it doesn't keep us from experiencing heartbreak in our lives from relationships that have not worked out. But when you've been physically intimate in your relationship and it ends, there is a different and deeper kind of pain that is experienced. Why? Because it is the unavoidable consequence of acting contrary to what God calls us to. God never intended for us to share ourselves intimately with someone by giving the deepest part of ourselves away without the sincerest possible commitment. In its most basic sense, sex is too profound an experience to be diminished and shared without meaning or outside of the context for which it was created.

Despite today's accepted sexual norms and influences, as Catholic singles, we are called to live differently, and this includes living chastely. Even when sexually pressured by society, friends, or the person we are dating, we are called to live according to God's laws, which are more often than not at odds with the world's mores. At times, we may feel alone in our choice of chastity, but Jesus teaches us that we never walk alone when we are walking with God. These are the times when we must place our hope and trust in God's promises to us, *especially* when we feel alone. St. Paul explains to us the importance of chastity and also reminds us of our inherent value as children of God:

> But he who is united to the Lord becomes one spirit with him. Shun immorality. Every other sin which a man commits is outside the body; but the immoral man sins against his own body. Do you not know that your body is a temple of the Holy Spirit within you, which you have from God? You are not your own; you were bought with a price. So glorify God in your body. (1 Cor. 6:17–20)

God wants the best for us, and He also wants us to imitate His Son. God's desire for us as single people, no matter what our age or life experiences, is to remain sexually and emotionally pure for marriage so we can experience the depth and beauty of the type of love He created from the beginning, which He called "good" (Gen. 1:31). After all, God invented sex, and it is meant to be an amazing gift between one man and one woman who have been united in a committed and sacramental bond. Therefore, the person we share this with should be someone we have committed to with the greatest discernment and care — because it is what true love requires. And while sex is something to be enjoyed, once it is offered prematurely outside of marriage, it ultimately hurts us.

Many Catholic singles are discouraged with today's dating scene and the pressure to sleep with someone just days, weeks, or at the most, months after knowing that person. Because "everyone else is doing it," many singles see it as part of the initial "getting to know you" phase of a relationship. This is where love becomes confused with lust and infatuation. Sex is meant to be the culmination of, not the introduction to, intimacy with another.

True love always considers what is best for the beloved. It means that if we truly love someone, we want what is best for the beloved beyond ourselves and our desires. The whole idea behind dating is not to hook up but to look for that person we can commit ourselves to for the rest of our lives. Consequently, it is imperative to be more discerning about this life-changing choice than at any other time in our lives.

There is no point in pursuing a relationship with someone if that person does not equally understand how important your beliefs are to you. It's important to let others know early on while dating that you plan to remain chaste and why. The person you are dating might understand when you explain it, even if he or she has not been exposed to this way of thinking. This is how God might be using you to reach others. If, however, someone you have been honest with from the beginning dismisses your desires later on in the relationship, what that person is really telling you is that he or she cannot be trusted in this way and perhaps in other ways.

When you are dating, either casually or seriously, avoiding the slippery slope can be tricky, especially if you are falling in love with your partner and have been dating a while. This is when it's important to avoid situations that might lead to sexual temptation. Obviously, the call to chastity does not apply only to women — it applies also to men.

Prayer, namely, through having a very close relationship with the Blessed Virgin Mary, is the greatest tool that men and women have when it comes to remaining chaste. The reason for this is that the Blessed Virgin allowed God to shine through her as a human to relate to us in a way that is completely pure. It's the same thing with women. When women allow themselves to go down the slippery slope of sex, it is ultimately because they want to be loved—and so they feel as if they have to give up more—but deep down, what they are really seeking is to be loved.

Therefore, in seeking to be loved, we may at times act too much with our heart and not enough with our head and even disregard the promptings of our soul. In other words, when we sleep with someone prior to marriage, it has a tendency to take away our objectivity and clarity about the relationship. Not only does it cloud our judgment and complicate matters, but it also hinders us from focusing on falling in love for all the right reasons while also remaining objective enough to discern whether this person is the one for us.

When we are sexually intimate before marriage, we deny ourselves and our new spouse the mystery that comes with being newlyweds and beginning our marriage with the most profound and binding act of love. Because it is meant for this, when we are sexually active before marriage, we may feel that bond and enter mentally and emotionally into a quasi-marital union that can be deeply destructive and may well end in heartbreak. Worse, we can end up with a "been there, done that" attitude that only reinforces society's cavalier attitude about sexuality and the sacredness of marital union.

It's also important to find others who share and embrace the Catholic teachings on chastity. Surrounding yourself with friends and people who share your Catholic values and Faith is very important. It's important to remember that sexual intimacy can skew your perception of a relationship, which may include disregarding red flags. When you find someone who could be your future spouse, it's important to establish a prayer life as a couple that is either engaged or dating. This can really help overcome any temptations. You might find that you share particular devotions and it's never a bad idea to spend time in adoration as a couple.

Fortunately, more and more people are realizing that sex isn't the answer to life's problems. In fact, sex outside of marriage creates more problems than it solves. Truly intimate relationships have been replaced with recreational sex without strings that leads individuals to view their partners as objects to be used rather than viewing them as future spouses. Therefore, couples who become sexually involved prior to a marriage can waste months or even years on a relationship that isn't going anywhere.

Chastity is about so much more than virginity, and it applies to men and women alike. With the onslaught of pornography and easy sex, people can become desensitized to the point where they view others only as objects or feel it is appropriate to use someone else's body strictly for pleasure. Men have been particularly targeted socially to feel entitled to live in this manner.

Equally inconsistent with today's culture is the idea that women have a significant responsibility when it comes to keeping things on a healthy moral track in relationships. Venerable Archbishop Fulton Sheen, the great televangelist and prolific author, articulates how women can have a tremendous impact and influence when it comes to men:

> To a great extent the level of any civilization is the level of its womanhood. When a man loves a woman, he has to become worthy of her. The higher her virtue, the more noble her character, the more devoted she is to truth,

justice, goodness—the more a man has to aspire to be worthy of her. The history of civilization could actually be written in terms of *the level of its women.*[34]

In contrast to today's hookup culture, Archbishop Sheen's words send a powerful message to women the world over that encourages us to embrace virtuous living heroically and thereby set the standard for civilization as a whole. In this way, women can "to a great extent" have a strong impact when it comes to ennobling men to strive for greater character, virtue, truth, justice, and goodness.

Yet our culture does little to acknowledge our true value as daughters of God. On the contrary, we are encouraged to compromise our values and our inherent dignity in order to feel valued and loved while setting ourselves up for abandonment, betrayal, and heartache. In failing to recognize our worth as "more precious than jewels" (Prov. 3:15) in the eyes of God, we forsake the opportunity to grow in personal holiness and at the same time deny the men in our lives something to aspire to.

Although there are already many women leading virtuous lives, there are many who stray from what God wishes for us as well as some who have no idea what we are called to live. Consequently, so many are suffering the pain and confusion of living outside of God's will. When this happens, the opportunity to set the bar higher for men is only lowered each time women give themselves sexually outside of marriage. Archbishop Sheen tells us that God has placed the desire deep within the hearts of men to find someone who challenges them to greater virtue,

[34] Fulton J. Sheen, *Life Is Worth Living* (San Francisco: Ignatius Press, 1999), 123.

goodness, and holiness and with whom they feel they are the luckiest guy in the world.

Archbishop Sheen also continually pointed to Mary as the perfect example for women to follow as a role model. By looking to Mary, the Mother of God, and finding in her the secret of living our true femininity with dignity and personal spiritual advancement, we can also inspire the men in our lives to embrace a more noble, virtuous, and faith-filled way of living and loving. Contrary to the message of our culture and media, a sexual climate that centers on our self-gratification is not the key to happiness.

Our culture has thrown away all morality, with many people choosing to live a sort of "fast food life": they want a relationship and intimacy with someone *now* — not a relationship that takes time to mature and grow, but *now*, up to and including an intimate relationship before marriage. On a practical level, it's not worth giving up that very sacred part of your being for someone else for an instant, fleeting moment of pleasure.

So, what if you have failed in the quest to remain chaste? Now is the time to go to Confession, ask for God's forgiveness and start over. We are a sinful people, and we can only begin again, humbler and wiser. If nothing else, the experience should reaffirm the wisdom behind following the path we are called to.

In present times, it is easy to see why many young, and not so young, Christians confronted by the sexual immorality all around us find it difficult to remain pure. Inevitably, much of our lives are about growing as the result of our mistakes and having learned from them. So when we fall, whether it be through human weakness or yielding to pressure from friends, society, or our significant other, it's important always to remember that we can return to chaste living knowing that God can take our biggest mistakes and bring goodness out of them. If we are truly repentant and resolve to "go and do no sin again" (John 8:11), God in His endless mercy is able to renew and restore us.

Although we're not likely to hear much about it in the news, a growing number of men and women are choosing to remain chaste until marriage. A sexual "retro-revolt" of sorts seems to be taking shape across the United States, with many young adults signing public pledges of virginity, wearing purity rings, and taking part in programs across the country that ask teens to pledge to remain virgins until marriage. According to a 2011 report issued by the Centers for Disease Control and Prevention's National Center for Health Statistics, researchers found that between 2006 and 2008, the percentage of fifteen- to twenty-four-year-old men who had never had any form of sexual contact with another person was 27 percent (up from 22 percent in 2002), and the percentage of fifteen- to twenty-four-year-old females who had never had any sex whatsoever was 29 percent (up from 22 percent in 2002).[35]

For a variety of reasons, adults of all ages are starting to realize that they've been sold a pack of lies when it comes to sex outside of marriage and are instead finding happiness, freedom, and contentment in adopting a chaste lifestyle. So whether you have always been chaste or have recently chosen to return to living chastely, your decision to do so will be one of the best decisions you've ever made.

[35] Anjani Chandra, William D. Mosher, Casey Copen, and Catlainn Sionean, "Sexual Behavior, Sexual Attraction, and Sexual Identity in the United States: Data From the 2006–2008 National Survey of Family Growth," National Health Statistics Reports, no. 36, March 3, 2011, http://www.cdc.gov/nchs/data/nhsr/nhsr036.pdf.

10

Single but Not Alone!

Throughout this book we have discussed the many challenges we face as Catholic singles and the importance of embracing our life in the *here and now* while remaining open to God's will and His plan for our future. Any other way of living would deny the importance of our present lives and leave God out of bringing the best that He has in store for us. We are, however, still left with the ever-present reality that we are only human, and this means that inevitably we are all going to have a bad day from time to time. There may also be times when we find ourselves downright sad, anxious, or in an emotional funk for a myriad of reasons — including because we are single! But what then? What can we do when we find ourselves in this particular state of mind?

Although being single does have its benefits, including free reign over the remote control and plenty of closet space, we experience that undeniable loneliness that can be triggered by any number of things. If we are not careful, we can find ourselves on a slippery slope that leads us into an unhealthy emotional landscape filled with all kinds of anxious thoughts and fears. These thoughts are especially tough to overcome for those of us who still wish to be married and have a family. We might battle with thoughts of how others of our age are now married with children and wonder why this hasn't happened yet for us. Or we might anxiously wonder, "What will become of me if I remain permanently single?"

The holidays can be especially tough. Although it may seem cliché, waking up on Christmas morning to a silence we generally appreciate might instead strike us as a sign of isolation and a stark reminder that we are not surrounded by the family we may have hoped for. Such times may also lead us toward feeling unloved, unworthy of love, or simply unlucky in love. This is exactly the kind of scary, dangerous, and useless thinking I am talking about watching out for! If we continue to entertain such thoughts, we may also be tempted to consider that because we don't have a family of our own, we somehow lack purpose in the whole "circle of life" way of looking at things.

Inevitably, such a negative outlook is not good for any of us on a number of levels, and this brings us right back to addressing one of the major points we have been exploring this entire time. It is imperative that we not give in to or even consider the thought that if only we were married with children, we would somehow have greater value in the eyes of the world and in the eyes of God. Wishing we were someplace other than where we are *now* in life or thinking that somehow we've been ripped off compared with other folks in God's plan because we're still single is the sure path to despair and bitterness. Then we are useless to ourselves and everyone else. Giving in is not an option! We might struggle with difficult moments and emotions, but we need to work through them so as to emerge on the other side and ultimately become victorious over such unproductive thoughts, which serve only to drain our peace and joy.

Far from ignoring such feelings or pretending to the outside world that we're "just fine," we need to face our negative thoughts and emotions, identify them for what they are, and deal directly with them. As always, it is best to step back, take a deep breath, and set about addressing first things first. We need to take a time out and realize that we are not really alone and that God is always with us (see Matt. 28:20). We can take great comfort in knowing that God, who specifically calls us to "fear not" (Luke 12:7), has it all under control, even in the midst of the particular anxieties and concerns that can confront us as singles. As Catholics, we have been given the profound gift of being able to call God "Father." Like a good Father, He knows his children intimately, including knowing what we need before we even ask! When we do not like the way things are going, however, we might be inclined to ask God, "What about me?" We might feel as if God has abandoned us or that we aren't even on His radar. In other cases, we may begin to question our beliefs or seek answers to our dilemma elsewhere.

If we live our Faith as Jesus teaches us, though, and find ways to short-circuit our loneliness and hopelessness, we may come to learn how God is "our refuge and strength, a very present help in trouble" (Ps. 46:1). It's the goal we need to keep aiming for, and God shows us how we can do this. His only requirement is that we submit ourselves *wholly* to His will while *trusting* in His divine providence when it comes to all aspects of our lives. However, if we nervously anticipate what the future will bring instead of just trusting in God *today* by living in the present moment, we are only setting ourselves up for the kind of negative emotions that cause us worry, pain, and hopelessness. When such moments of anxiety and perhaps even depression come, it is important to tackle them immediately; as such emotions are inevitably useless and actually dangerous for our state of mind, our overall physical health, and our very souls. Consequently, it is well worth every effort to fight against these emotions that prove over and over again that they are not our friends.

Naturally, we all experience loneliness from time to time. Jesus, too, experienced loneliness. Imagine the loneliness He felt when Peter, whom He had ordained as the Rock of His Church, denied Him not once, but three times, claiming, "I do not know the man" (Matt. 26:72); or during His agony in the Garden of Gethsemane, when His disciples couldn't stay awake to accompany Him in prayer. Most of all—imagine the unspeakable depth of loneliness He felt on the Cross during His abandonment, when in freedom and love he "offered his life to his Father through the Holy Spirit in reparation for our disobedience" (CCC 614).

In our lives, the most difficult and negative emotions we experience are meant to motivate us and help us appreciate their opposite state. Loneliness, therefore, should motivate us and make us aware of the value of others. It should also help us recognize our profound interconnectedness and push us out into the world to seek others and also experience the joys, challenges, and sacrifice in valuing others beyond ourselves. This is a good and wonderful thing, as all things can be good, if God is at the center of our lives!

Remember that when we are far from God, we are vulnerable. Therefore, our best defense, as always, is a good offense. We must do our very best to make sure we always continue to focus on our relationship with God, knowing that He is always near us and desires to be involved in our lives. However, we will not be able to recognize His providential hand in our lives if we are disconnected from Him and are living in such a way that He cannot enter because the door to our hearts has been closed.

It is also important to recognize the difference between being lonely and choosing to be alone. In our fast-paced and sometimes frantic world, we can recognize and appreciate how much we singles value our alone time. When I get home from work, I am often grateful for the time I have to unwind in a way that suits me as opposed to those who may go home to be immediately hit with the needs of a family. That is a perfect example of finding joy in our life. Likewise, the father who heads home after a long day at the office and has to take his son to Boy Scouts before he has a chance to change out of his business suit is also called to find the joy in his circumstances.

It is healthy to step back for a while and learn the lessons that can be found only in silence. It is often easier for us singles to find that silence than those who are married and have families, and we should appreciate the opportunity for what it can be. In addition, we must always take care not to isolate ourselves while appreciating and taking advantage of the opportunities we have for quiet time and meditation.

While we can be very busy in our single lives, there is also the opposite danger of having entirely too much time on our hands to think about ourselves. That is the temptation we must always be on guard against, because many of us aren't given the opportunity in our personal lives to stretch and make the accommodations that those who are married with children are called to do every day. It is like the difference between those who do a lot of physical labor for their work and those who have to go to the gym to stay fit because of less physically demanding jobs. Of course, we can take things to an extreme and become fixated on our loneliness, but this often tends to breed discouragement if we choose to do nothing about it. It can be compared to sitting on a couch watching TV with our second package of Oreos and then feeling miserable and unwell because we are unhealthy and out of shape. Similarly, when we become fixated on our solitude, become too self-oriented, or choose to isolate ourselves beyond what is healthy, we need to spend some one-on-one time with God and ask His help in reorienting ourselves to a healthier lifestyle and emotional balance. We might find benefit in seeking outside help from a Catholic counselor or spiritual director. We can also find great comfort and hope through Adoration. According to St. Alphonsus Liguori, "Of all devotions, that of adoring Jesus in the Blessed Sacrament is the greatest after the sacraments, the one dearest to God, and the one most helpful to us."[36]

Most of all, we need to remember that God is always at the helm of our lives, even if we sometimes don't fully understand where He is steering the ship. When this happens, we need to trust in God and then get busy doing something positive in our lives including simply enjoying the day and the people God has given us. Whenever we get discouraged, that is the perfect time for prayer. It is when we look at Christ that we are reminded that He has already overcome the world's darkness. So, we must stay close to Christ, especially in the Eucharist, where His comforting presence is palpable. For the Catholic single, this is our greatest source of intimacy and friendship, especially in a culture where it is really hard to find community among likeminded Catholics who are also trying to live the Gospel.

Ironically, in a world that is more connected than ever through digital communications, more and more people are feeling disconnected. While social-networking sites are extremely popular, one-on-one conversations are being replaced in favor of "connecting" with others we've never actually met in person.

---

[36] Alcuin Reid, *From Eucharistic Adoration to Evangelization* (London: Burns and Oates, 2012), 130.

It's a great way to reach others we might not otherwise reach, but we are simultaneously losing touch with the truly meaningful relationships with those who are right around us. In a report in *The Atlantic*, writer Stephen Marche looked into the extensive use of social-network sites and what it is doing to our souls and society. According to Marche, while "social media — from Facebook to Twitter — have made us more densely connected than ever ... new research suggests that we have never been lonelier."[37]

Featured in Marche's article is John Cocioppo, director of the Center for Cognitive and Social Neuroscience at the University of Chicago. A leading expert on loneliness, Cocioppo notes that "the greater the proportion of face-to-face interactions, the less lonely you are ... the greater the proportion of online interaction, the lonelier you are." Cocioppo also stressed that the use of social-media sites such as Facebook can become unhealthy when it begins to replace in-person interactions. "If social media lets you organize a game of football among your friends, that's healthy," says Cocioppo. "If you turn to social media instead of playing football, however, that's unhealthy." So while such networking sites can be great for some things, including the evangelization of others, posting uplifting thoughts, and simply touching base, we also need to be careful that our "super-connectedness" isn't, in fact, inviting more loneliness.

Beyond seeking temporal help and support as well as reaching out to friends and family, how else can we combat loneliness? Jesus Himself provides the most powerful way of combating the loneliness that can come in being single. When we receive the

[37] Stephen Marche, "Is Facebook Making Us Lonely?" *Atlantic*, May 2012, accessed July 17, 2015, http://www.theatlantic.com/magazine/archive/2012/05/is-facebook-making-us-lonely/308930/.

Holy Eucharist, "the source and summit of the Christian life" (CCC 1324), it is Jesus who gives us the life-giving strength we need to move forward and find fulfillment, no matter what our state or vocation. Father Lawrence Lovasik, founder of the Sisters of the Divine Spirit and author of *The Basic Book of the Eucharist* writes beautifully on finding strength through the Holy Eucharist:

> Holy Communion will afford you great consolation in all the sorrows and sufferings of this earthly life. No matter how great your need and your trouble may be, no matter if all forsake you, Christ will never fail you. How could you doubt Him who became man and died on the Cross for you and who gave Himself to be your daily food? At Holy Communion, there is opened to you a world of life, light, and love, a gracious outpouring of the treasures of the Sacred Heart of Jesus, the Fount of all grace, holiness, and Christian joyfulness. At this fount of joy you will find the strength and courage to undertake great things for God's glory and the welfare of your neighbor.[38]

Beyond the sacrament of the Holy Eucharist and the healing power of the sacrament of Reconciliation are those "sacred signs which bear a resemblance to the sacraments" (CCC 1667) known as sacramentals, from which we can also draw strength and consolation. According to the *Catechism of the Catholic Church*, "sacramentals are sacred signs instituted by the Church. They prepare us to receive the fruit of the sacraments and sanctify different circumstances of life" (CCC 1677). They are those

---

[38] Lawrence Lovasik, *The Basic Book of the Eucharist* (Manchester, NH: Sophia Institute Press, 2001), 134.

"little extras" we can draw encouragement from and that can also serve as reminders of the blessings of our Faith, not only for ourselves but also as a sign of our Faith to others. Sacramentals include making the Sign of the Cross, receiving ashes on Ash Wednesday, and the sprinkling of holy water, as well as many popular devotions that are unique to our Faith and can contribute to our spiritual growth and peace.

We discussed earlier perhaps the most popular and well-known Catholic devotion: the Holy Rosary. It is a devotion that one beautiful jewelry designer has found particular strength in as a single. It also reminds us of the unselfish choice that our Blessed Mother Mary made when she said yes to the will of God.

Being single can be very difficult at times. It is very easy to think about how lonely *I* am; why no one seems to be the right fit for *me*; when is it going to be *my* turn; et cetera. Praying the Rosary involves surrendering to our current situation and accepting the single life with gratitude. Through it we can find that the most satisfying relationship is the one that we nurture with Jesus Christ while we contemplating His life, death, and Resurrection. After all, our Blessed Mother Mary wants just that—that we grow closer to her Son.

Beyond finding strength and comfort through the sacraments, sacramentals, and devotions such as the Rosary to battle the aloneness we sometimes feel as singles, it is important that we also seek other ways in which to get outside of ourselves. It is up to us to work to maintain our connections with those we most value in our lives. It is also important to step out and try new things in an effort to increase our relationships and interactions with others. Whether it is attending a Catholic singles conference or a singles retreat, becoming active in our local parish, volunteering, or just being more social in our daily lives, we are all personally responsible in making the choice to stop being lonely. Saying yes to the Lord and being open to letting Him work in our lives is the best way of doing this, along with knowing that our plans always pale in comparison with His! We are all called to bloom where we are planted and not to wait for some other time or some other place or situation to do so. We must also remind ourselves that God's supreme goal for us is not necessarily our immediate earthly happiness but rather our sanctification, so that we can be with Him forever in heaven. So, whenever you feel down due to loneliness or discouragement, remember that God is acting in your life toward this end. Remember also that He loves you immeasurably and that with His love you are never alone.

11

Keeping the Faith

Throughout this book we have journeyed together through the many challenges we face as single Catholics today. We've examined the powerful force for good we can be, not only for those whose lives we might touch, but also for our Church and the world at large. We've explored the reasons why staying true to our Faith is crucial to remaining true to who we are and to realizing God's plan for our lives. Since our Faith is our foundation, it is only by using this compass that we can make decisions in our lives that will lead us to realize all God wants us to become. We've also recognized, I hope, the deep importance of supporting and encouraging each other while seeking personally to live our Faith more fully. Some of us may have never left this path, and some of us may be finding our way back. Regardless, all that matters is that we continue to persevere.

In addition, we've explored how the world is deeply in need of people of action and conviction who are willing to stand up for their Faith against all the forces that attempt to deceive us—not only through our words and actions, but also through the example of daily living that reflects the truth and defends Church teachings. As Catholic singles, we are in a wonderful and unique position to be a rallying force in today's world, which offers, at best, confused versions of happiness and fleeting pleasures that fail to satisfy.

If you believe that marriage is between one man and one woman and that life is sacred from the moment of conception until natural death; and if you don't buy into today's hookup culture but instead choose to remain chaste until marriage — this pretty much makes you a rebel amid current cultural norms. This rebellion, however, is something to celebrate and to acknowledge as a revolution that is both just and courageous! By going against current cultural trends, digging deeper into your Faith, and taking a stand for Church teachings, you are part of a remnant of faithful and faith-filled single Catholics living in the world today. It is often lonely and difficult; it also requires great insight and fortitude, yet there isn't anything else we are doing that is as profoundly important.

There is no doubt that we are living in difficult times — and the battle lines are made clearer with each passing day. Someone needs to remain an example of what the truth can lead us to become. At our Baptism we were called to be a *light in the world* (cf. Matt. 5:14). Whether we are twenty, forty, or seventy years old, we are all called to be God's hands, feet, eyes, and words in a world that thirsts for the unconditional love, mercy, peace, and goodness that can be found only in Christ and through faith in God. The second letter of Timothy speaks well to the current times and tells us how we should live in response: "For the time is coming when people will not endure sound teaching, but having itching ears they will accumulate for themselves teachers to suit their own likings, and will turn away from listening to the truth and wander into myths. As for you, always be steady, endure suffering, do the work of an evangelist, fulfil your ministry" (2 Tim. 4:3–5).

Keeping the Faith

Therefore, we must ask ourselves how we are living our lives. Are we fulfilling our ministry as Catholic singles in the here and now? Are we using the unique gifts and talents that God has given us in achieving the personal mission that only we can accomplish during our time on earth? Living your life in obedience to the Church's teachings is *hard*, but it is the right way to live, and you can know its rewards only when you actually *do* it. It is a life-changing choice.

To live as a faithful Catholic is our first vocation, and as with all vocations, we must expect to experience hardship. As I noted at the beginning of the book — there's no point in candy-coating our situation. There are times in our single lives when we have difficulties that may bring us to our knees, but we must remember that when we suffer, whatever it is that we suffer, whether it is loneliness, spiritual dryness, temptation, physical illness, rejection, or anything else in the whole long list of challenges we might face, God can make these negative experiences have a positive outcome, if we let Him.

God can transform all things for good when we accept His grace and allow Him to work in our lives in addition to remaining obedient to His commandments and the guidelines given to us through the Church. If we should fail, we must get up and start again, and yet again, until we prevail. In addition, we must always remember to take advantage of the great gift we have in always being able to start anew through the sacrament of Reconciliation. Ultimately, the most valuable and important lessons of our life will always lead to the most profound lesson of all: that God's love is the only love that can truly satisfy us.

The world desperately needs men and women who are informed and on fire with love and zeal for Christ and His Church. As singles, our vocation is to cooperate with God's grace in our daily lives. Bishop Robert Gruss, of the Diocese of Rapid City, also emphasizes that if we are truly living our Faith in today's world, it involves a sort of martyrdom when we commit to going against the tide of secularization and standing up for our Faith, even if it requires that we stand alone. "If we are not praying," Bishop Gruss warns, "we will float along with the culture and fall into the ways of the world." In rooting ourselves in prayer, we cling to the Truth that seeks to put us on the right path. Bishop Gruss concludes:

> You need to be a martyr in the world today to live your faith. With all the secularization of today's world — martyrdom is required. It's standing up for what we believe in. It's about becoming and living as an authentic disciple without counting the costs. If we are living our lives the way Jesus calls us to — there is a cost. We do it because we know that our relationship with the Lord depends upon it and our salvation depends upon it.

Many of you know the kind of martyrdom Bishop Gruss speaks of. It is the daily martyrdom of living our Catholic Faith in a world that is increasingly opposed to its teachings. Therefore, we must anticipate that when we stand in the Faith, we will suffer. Yet, despite the times in which we live, single or not, God calls each of us to be saints. In fact, it has never been more important for us to prove by our example that there is a way to live other than the way of the world.

The secular world will tell us that sanctity is an impossible goal and not even one worth striving for, while it simultaneously beckons us to take the wider, easier path. Consequently, it takes great courage and fortitude to live in the world, but not of the world (see John 15:19; Rom. 12:2). The choice to live our Faith, however, will always be its own reward because it is the surest way to happiness and the only way to everlasting life. We only need to entrust ourselves to God, look to Church teachings for guidance, fortify ourselves through the sacraments, and call upon, God, Mary, and the saints for support.

In addition, there can be no greater response to the times in which we live than that of being joyful—the consistent mark of Christianity. That is why we are called to embrace our single circumstances, *especially* when it isn't exactly what some of us might have hoped for. It's easy to keep the Faith in good times, but what about those periods of great challenge? This is when and how saints are formed—in the call for patient endurance when we keep choosing God again and again, no matter the trial. Naturally, there will be times when we get discouraged, and that is when it is imperative to remind ourselves that we are living for something much bigger.

It is also important to stop for a moment and recognize just how remarkable you are in living the Faith fully in today's world or even seeking to live it more fully. I commend those who continue to walk courageously in the Faith, despite the promptings of a world, which calls us to live otherwise. You wouldn't even be reading this book if you didn't care deeply about your relationship with God. If you are trying to find a more fulfilling way to live or if you are trying to begin again in your faith journey, know that you are doing a great work and you are amazing!

So often people live and judge their lives by whether they've hit their marks—obtaining a college degree in their early twenties; establishing themselves in a career by their thirties; or getting married and starting a family by a particular age. Yet God calls us to measure our lives in a different way, by urging us to look instead at how we enter into the present moment and how much love we are putting into that moment. Therefore, the fullness of life is about recognizing the gifts we have in the *here and now*. This means recognizing the true value of our relationships, our family, our friends, our colleagues, and the powerful gift of our Faith and in being members of Christ's universal Church.

Some of us can also get caught up in a relentless pursuit of professional prestige. As the famous phrase from Paul Tsongas states "Nobody on their deathbed has ever said, 'I wish I had spent more time at the office.' "[39] At the end of our lives, we will instead remember the times we spent with family and friends, the love that we have shared with others, and the service we have given. If there is one message I can reaffirm as a fellow Catholic single, it is this: the secret to living as a joyful, Catholic single is accepting where you are in life and making the most of every day that is given to you.

Pope Francis recently said, "The world tells us to seek success, power and money. God tells us to seek humility, service and love."[40] Therefore, it is important to remember that when we have God, we lack nothing. If you have left the Church and are single, I invite you to reconsider and join me and other Catholic singles across the globe in rediscovering the richness and beauty of our Faith. If you have never married, or are divorced, widowed, or a single parent, it's important for all of us to remind ourselves, especially when we feel alone, that we are never really alone. We

---

[39] Paul Tsongas, *The Dictionary of Modern Proverbs*, ed. Charles Clay Doyle, Wolfgang Mieder, Fred R. Shapairo (New Haven: Yale University Press, 2012), 52.

[40] Scot Landry, "Top 10 Tweets from Pope Francis' First Seven Months," *Pilot*, October 18, 2013, accessed July 17, 2015, http://www.thebostonpilot.com/article.asp?ID=16538.

have God, and we are all part of the global family that is the one, holy, catholic, and apostolic Church.

Now is the time for us to "take the whole armor of God" (Eph. 6:13) to help us resist the temptations and evils of our time, to live fully in the present moment, to cultivate an active faith, and to share it with others. As singles, we can be tremendous warriors of God and the Church in today's world through our generous and obedient response to His grace. Then with confidence we can say, "I have fought the good fight, I have finished the race, I have kept the faith" (2 Tim. 4:7).

12

The Perfect Destination Wedding

When considering marriage, it is important to remember that while we may dream of the perfect wedding, what we're really aiming for is finding that special someone whom God has chosen for us. With the overemphasis on weddings these days, it sometimes seems as if it is more about finding the right venue than the right person. However, when we think we have found the right one or if we are simply just dreaming of our big day, it is important to recognize, as Catholics, why the Church is the best place to exchange our vows. You will go to Mass often and pray for the right spouse while you learn to live your life in Christ. So, why not consider how this Church is a perfect spot to discern marriage as well as what that means for you?

It seems as if weddings these days are being held everywhere but in churches. With destination weddings being all the rage, more couples are opting for nuptials that are performed beachside, poolside, atop mountains, or at Tuscan-like villas reproduced specifically for weddings and receptions, just to name a few of the numerous popular alternatives.

According to recent statistics from the Center for Applied Research in the Apostolate (CARA), there has been a significant decrease in the number of Catholic couples seeking to marry within the Church. CARA cites that in 1970, there were more than 426,000 couples in the United States that were married in the Catholic Church. However, even though the U.S. Catholic population has dramatically increased since the seventies, Catholic marriages have declined dramatically. In 2014, just over 154,000 couples were married in the Church.[41]

The reasons couples are choosing to marry outside the Church are as varied as the number of designer wedding gowns. One of the most common justifications is that many couples feel God is just as present on the shores of a beautiful coastline or atop a scenic vista as in a church. Others decide that destination weddings are simply more convenient and economical since they are able to have their marriage, reception, and even their honeymoon in the same place. In addition, there are those who feel that marrying outside the Church means there are fewer hoops to jump through. Sadly, many couples have taken God out of the equation altogether in favor of self-written wedding vows and Internet-sanctioned officiants. Whatever the reasons may be, there is a notable trend among Christians to marry outside the four walls of their local parish church.

Many people would agree that weddings have steadily become more and more extravagant and nontraditional. Statistics certainly support that observation. Carol McD. Wallace, author of the book *All Dressed in White: The Irresistible Rise of the American Wedding*, notes, "When *Brides* magazine debuted in 1934, and after World War II, the boom in marriages kicked the wedding

---

[41] "Frequently Requested Church Statistics," "United States Data over Time: Sacramental Marriages," Center for Applied Research in the Apostolate (CARA) website, accessed May 11, 2015, http://cara.georgetown.edu/CARAServices/requested-churchstats.html.

industry into high gear. But in the 1960s and '70s, many young couples steeped in countercultural disdain for displays of wealth and status chose simpler ceremonies. Then in 1981, the lavish wedding came roaring back in two words: 'Princess Diana.' "[42]

Prior to the royal wedding of Prince Charles and Princess Diana, steeped in all its magnificent regalia, the majority of weddings were comparatively simple affairs by today's standards. It was a given that vows were usually exchanged in church and receptions were usually held in the church basement or at some other low-key location. Far different from today's typical raucous blowout events that begin with deejay-orchestrated entrances of fist-pumping newlyweds bounding into ballrooms to the beat of hip-hop music so the "real party" can begin.

Unlike the simple ceremonies of the past, weddings, it seems, have become stressful extravaganzas rather than sacred lifetime events to be commemorated. Of course, a wedding is an important event in one's life that deserves preparation and consideration, but not to the exclusion or exhaustion of remembering the real point of the day—entering into a lifelong covenant while remaining open to the creation of new life. Nowadays, brides-to-be agonize over the perfect dress, extravagant floral arrangements, whom to invite, whom not to invite, exorbitant catering fees, wedding-day photos, the wedding cake, the perfect knife to cut it with, and the list goes on!

In addition, the wedding is often focused so exclusively on the bride and the happenings of *her* big day that the guys appear to be sidelined, with husbands-to-be seeming almost incidental

[42] "The Wedding Industrial Complex," *The Week*, June 15, 2013, accessed July 16, 2015, http://theweek.com/articles/463257/wedding-industrial-complex.

to the whole process. Is it just to get a guy, so you can have the wedding? Then what? Shouldn't this be about the woman *and* the man? Shouldn't both people in this marriage be equally important? Is it any wonder that amid all this it becomes more about the wedding and very little about the actual marriage?

This is certainly not the case with all marriages, but it is a valid observation when you consider that according to global market research firm IBISWorld, wedding services in the United States alone generated fifty-five billion dollars in revenue in 2014.[43] But this trend is not likely one the consumer culture would be motivated to curb. If a wedding even occurs in a church, it often seems as if the altar serves merely as a backdrop to the ceremony. In fact, the wedding ceremony itself is often relegated to nothing more than a necessary formality before the "real fun" of the reception gets underway. Has marriage become another casualty of our consumerist society that places so much value on the secular and so little on the sacred? This conjecture does not seem too far off the mark, given our celebrity-centric pop culture, featuring "A-List Star" weddings, essentially bought and paid for by advertisers or celebrity magazines seeking exclusive photo rights, that frequently end in equally well-publicized divorce.

Although God is indeed present always and everywhere, including in nature, somewhere along the way a growing number of couples have decided to overlook the profound and sacred act of a traditional church wedding to focus instead on what has "personal meaning" for them without fully comprehending the truth behind the tradition. I speak of the teachings of our

---

[43] "Wedding Services in the U.S.; Market Research Report," IBIS-World, November 2014, accessed July 16, 2015, http://www.ibisworld.com/industry/default.aspx?indid=2008.

Faith that have been seriously deliberated and discerned before they even became traditions within the Church. Such traditions, drawn directly from Christ's teachings, are deeply profound and full of meaning.

So no matter where you are in your search for your soul mate, it is equally important to do some serious soul searching *now* about the level of commitment that an impending marriage involves and the reasons the Church asks us, as Catholics, to understand the sacrament fully and enter into it in a holy and obedient way.

Most likely the decline in Catholic weddings is not only the result of cultural influences but can also be attributed to young people's poor understanding of their Catholic Faith and why it is important to wed in the Church. So let's look at the reasons the Church believes it is so important that couples join in Matrimony at the altar of their parish church.

In the sacrament of Matrimony, a baptized Christian man and a baptized Christian woman exchange vows before God, promising to each other a love that is faithful, permanent, exclusive, self-sacrificing, and life-giving. According to the *Catechism of the Catholic Church*, "since marriage establishes the couple in a public state of life in the Church, it is fitting that its celebration be public in the framework of a liturgical celebrations, before the priest (or a witness authorized by the Church), the witnesses [usually the best man and the maid of honor] and the assembly of the faithful," who have gathered for the ceremony (cf. CCC 1663).

Regardless of how you found your way into the Catholic Church, as a believer in Christ, you should seek to be married in the Church. After all, a church is consecrated ground; the altar is also consecrated through a sacred and solemn rite. It is the holiest and most sacred venue there could be, and it is where you've received other sacraments, including receiving Christ, truly present, in the Eucharist! Why would anyone want to exchange lifelong vows or have their wedding blessed and witnessed anywhere less sacred and holy than their church?

Oftentimes it is simply because they have not fully understood it for what it is. In contemplating the importance of marriage, Father Paul Sullivan states, "The vocation of marriage is ultimately a public statement of fidelity to each other and to God made within the Church." More importantly, marriage within the Church is the outpouring of God's graces upon the couple to allow them to live in lasting mutual fidelity. With such graces, what could be a better spot to celebrate this love than in the very place where moments of grace happen every day, such as Baptism, Confession, and the reception of Holy Communion? "Also," Fr Sullivan continues, "while couples tend not to return to the place of their destination wedding, those married in the Church return to that place of grace weekly, or even daily, to receive the support of God and the community."

The goal of the Church is to assist couples in discerning if they are truly right for one another and to ensure that every couple fully comprehends and carefully discerns the choice they are making before entering into a sacred and holy sacrament. It is a covenant bond and a vocation, no less important than that of any seminarian preparing for a vocation to the priesthood. This is why the Church sets the guidelines that a pastor and marriage-preparation team will use to help couples prepare themselves. Consequently, adequate time is necessary so that every couple is able to contemplate their decision fully and pray about making the right choice. As a concerned intermediary, the Church helps couples recognize just how important the decision to marry is and the permanent "till death do us part" level of commitment they are entering into before God. That is why the Church requires you to meet with the pastor and why you are required to take attend marriage-prep classes (sometimes called Pre-Cana classes), often taught by married couples. In other words, the Church wants your marriage to succeed!

Rosa and John, friends of mine who underwent marriage preparation in their parish, felt that their participation in marriage prep was important and will help them build a solid married life. "We both felt it was really valuable," says Rosa "It created conversation on all the important topics that, during a relationship, people sometimes neglect to discuss because it could be awkward. I think it really deepened our understanding of each other and our love for one another." Beyond the importance of marriage prep, the Church also believes that weddings are always a public event because the love between husband and wife is a visible sign that is representative of Jesus' love for His Bride, the Church.

Renee, a tall and effervescent forty-year-old woman employed as an occupational therapist, feels called to marriage and hopes to wed one day. Despite today's destination-wedding trend, Renee says it would be extremely important for her to marry in the Church, noting, "I absolutely want to have a sacramental marriage blessed by the Church! It's very important to me that I also marry someone who shares my values and to grow in holiness with my spouse, who will also attend Mass with me and share the same spiritual foundation on which to build a marriage. A sacramental marriage within the Church means we are also joined together spiritually. For me, if I am not married in the Church, I do not have that blessing of God."

You see, the sacraments make Christ present in our midst! But unlike the other sacraments, Marriage is not just for the good of our individual souls or for just the good of the couple but for the good of the entire community and the whole world! We marry in the Church because it is God's House. Jesus lives there. Yes, He lives in nature, at the beach, and so forth. But His Real Presence in the Eucharist is not reserved in the woods or at the beach. So what is it you are saying if you don't want to get married in front of the Real Presence of Jesus? This basically says, "Jesus, You're not a big part, if any, of my marriage." Plus, getting married in the Church is a communal act because the Church is made up of the People of God.

Their wedding day is one of the most important days in a couple's life, and certainly every couple wants their wedding to be memorable and personally significant. However, it can be all those things and more while being celebrated at your parish church. If you are Catholic without special permission from your bishop to marry elsewhere, you are called to marry in the Church, at the altar, before the Blessed Sacrament. This is not done to thwart a couple's aesthetic desires or to wield arbitrary power but because the Church has sound reasons that are solely meant for your spiritual welfare. The Church wedding may not always strike as glamorous, but it has all the details of God's presence. Those weddings to me are far more beautiful and much more satisfying than lavish weddings without Christ's presence.

Years ago there was a popular bumper sticker that said, "Loved the wedding, invite me to the marriage.—God." This phrase struck me because even when couples have had a traditional church wedding, they might fail to include God in their relationship once they are married. After the wedding flowers have faded, the dress has been stored away, and the honeymoon is literally and figuratively over—it is back to the daily realities of life. Together, you begin to face the actualities of marriage where the true call of sacrificial love begins. This is why it is important to realize that it actually takes *three* to make a marriage—you, your spouse, and God!

It is always possible that when we obediently and joyfully live our Faith, we may inspire others to join us in our Catholic journey as well. It's important to realize that your Catholic witness while dating, or in a marriage, may draw your partner into the Church. Many Catholics date baptized or unbaptized individuals who eventually decide to join the Faith as they come to a greater appreciation of what the Faith is and the grace it can bring into their lives. In a 2009 Pew Research Center study on religious conversion, 72 percent of adult Catholic converts said that marriage was an important factor in their decision to change their faith.[44] Therefore, just as Jesus taught us in the parable of the good tree bearing good fruit, we know that what is good leads to more of what is good. And isn't that all we could ever hope for in love and marriage?

[44] "Faith in Flux," Pew Research Center, last modified February 1, 2011, accessed July 16, 2015, http://www.pewforum.org/2009/04/27/faith-in-flux/

Resources

CATHOLIC FAITH

The Holy See
Official website: www.w2.vatican.va/content/vatican/en.html
Twitter: @HolySee & Pope Francis @Pontifex

United States Conference of Catholic Bishops (USCCB)
3211 Fourth Street NE, Washington, DC 20017
www.usccb.org
Twitter: @USCCB

Catechism of the Catholic Church
Online: www.vatican.va/archive/ENG0015/_INDEX.HTM
Twitter: @DailyCatechism

Catholic Answers
www.catholic.com
www.facebook.com/catholicanswers
Twitter: @catholiccom

Catholic Exchange
www.catholicexchange.com
www.facebook.com/catholicexchange
Twitter: @Cathexchange

Single and Catholic

Center for Applied Research in the Apostolate
www.cara.georgetown.edu
CARA@Georgetown.edu

Theology of the Body Institute
www.tobinstitute.org
info@tobinstitute.org
Twitter: @TOBinstitute

FELLOWSHIP AND SUPPORT GROUPS
Catholic Answers Chastity Outreach
www.chastity.com

Fellowship of Catholic University Students (FOCUS)
www.focus.org
info@focus.org
Twitter: @FOCUScatholic

National Catholic Singles Conference
www.nationalcatholicsingles.com

Catholic Alumni Clubs International
www.caci.org

The Catholic's Divorce Survival Guide
www.catholicsdivorce.com

Rose Sweet
Catholic Annulment Advocate
www.rosesweet.com
Twitter: @rosesweettweets

Resources

Covenant Eyes: Internet Accountability and Filtering
www.covenanteyes.com
info@covenanteyes.com
Toll-free in the US (877)479-1119
Twitter: @CovenantEyes

Proven Men Ministries
www.provenmen.org
Twitter: @PROVENMen

Rachel's Vineyard Ministry
www.rachelsvineyard.org
National Helpline for Abortion Recovery: 866-482-5433
For any man or woman who has struggled with the emotional and spirituals pain of abortion.

RIGHT TO LIFE

National Right to Life
www.nrlc.org
Twitter: @nrlc

American Life League
www.all.org
Twitter: @amerLifeLeague

Live Action
Founded by Lila Rose
www.liveaction.org
Twitter: @LiveActionFilms

Students for Life of America
www.studentsforlife.org
Twitter: @Students4LifeHQ

Single and Catholic

THE NEW EVANGELIZATION

Catholic Apostolate Center
www.catholicapostolatecenter.org
Twitter: @CathApostleCtr

Women in the New Evangelization (WINE)
www.womeninthenewevangelization.com

The New EMANgelization—Drawing Men to Jesus Christ
and His Catholic Church
www.newemangelization.com
Twitter: @eMANgelization

VOCATION DISCERNMENT

Vision Vocation Network
www.vocationnetwork.org
Vocation Action Circle, Inc.
www.vocation.com

Gods Call
www.gods-call.com

Father Donald Calloway, MIC
Vocation Director
Marians of the Immaculate Conception
www.marian.org/vocations
www.fathercalloway.com

The Diocese of Phoenix (Arizona)
Father Paul Sullivan
Director of Vocations
frsullivan@diocesephoenix.org
www.diocesephoenix.org/vocations-office
Twitter: @PhoenixPriest

Resources

Fr. Mark McCormick
Director of Vocations and Stewardship
The Diocese of Rapid City (South Dakota)
mmccormick@diorc.org
www.rapidcitydiocese.org/vocations

Fr. David Konderla
Director of Campus Ministry
Saint Mary's Catholic Center
Texas A&M University
dkonderla@aggiecatholic.org
www.aggiecatholic.org

CATHOLIC DATING WEBSITES
Catholic Match
www.catholicmatch.com
www.catholicmatch.com/institute

Ave Maria Singles
www.avemariasingles.com

Catholic Singles
www.catholicsingles.com

Saint Rafael Catholic Single
www.straphael.net

CATHOLIC DEVOTIONS AND BOOKS
The Secret of the Rosary, by St. Louis de Montfort
www.catholictradition.org/Classics/secret-rosary.htm

National Shrine of Divine Mercy
Marians of the Immaculate Conception
www.thedivinemercy.org

Single and Catholic

Sophia Institute Press
Box 5284, Manchester, NH 03108
www.sophiainstitute.com
Twitter: @SophiaInsPress

Forming Intentional Disciples — The Path to Knowing and Following Jesus, by Sherry A. Weddell (Our Sunday Visitor, 2012): recommended reading from Bishop Robert D. Gruss, Diocese of Rapid City

Judy Keane

Since 2012, Judy Keane has been a regular contributor to *Catholic Exchange*, where she writes on topics ranging from the saints to the single life. Judy is also an experienced marketing and communications professional and a former broadcast news producer for a major television affiliate. Internationally, she was involved in several foreign aid missions during the Balkan War and later returned to Bosnia-Herzegovina on sabbatical, where she worked as an English professor and in refugee camps for more than two years. She holds an MBA in International Business and a BA in English and humanities. Over the past decade, she has been an active member of the Arizona Marian Conference, where she has also served as a speaker and master of ceremonies. A lifelong Catholic, Judy resides in Phoenix, Arizona, and is single.

Sophia Institute

Sophia Institute is a nonprofit institution that seeks to nurture the spiritual, moral, and cultural life of souls and to spread the Gospel of Christ in conformity with the authentic teachings of the Roman Catholic Church.

Sophia Institute Press fulfills this mission by offering translations, reprints, and new publications that afford readers a rich source of the enduring wisdom of mankind.

Sophia Institute also operates two popular online Catholic resources: CrisisMagazine.com and CatholicExchange.com.

Crisis Magazine provides insightful cultural analysis that arms readers with the arguments necessary for navigating the ideological and theological minefields of the day. *Catholic Exchange* provides world news from a Catholic perspective as well as daily devotionals and articles that will help you to grow in holiness and live a life consistent with the teachings of the Church.

In 2013, Sophia Institute launched Sophia Institute for Teachers to renew and rebuild Catholic culture through service to Catholic education. With the goal of nurturing the spiritual, moral, and cultural life of souls, and an abiding respect for the role and work of teachers, we strive to provide materials and programs that are at once enlightening to the mind and ennobling to the heart; faithful and complete, as well as useful and practical.

Sophia Institute gratefully recognizes the Solidarity Association for preserving and encouraging the growth of our apostolate over the course of many years. Without their generous and timely support, this book would not be in your hands.

www.SophiaInstitute.com
www.CatholicExchange.com
www.CrisisMagazine.com
www.SophiaInstituteforTeachers.org

Celebrity Weddings
&
Honeymoon Getaways

ABOUT THE AUTHOR

Elizabeth Arrighi Borsting holds a degree in journalism from California State University, Long Beach, and is currently the public relations manager for the historic Queen Mary hotel and attraction. She and her husband Kurt reside in Long Beach, California.

Author's Note

When I was planning my own wedding a few years back, my fiancé and I made the usual site visits to properties where we were interested in having both our wedding and reception. In talking with our hosts, I learned Heather Locklear had married the first time at one location while John and Jacqueline Kennedy had honeymooned at another.

While I didn't want to seem caught up in the moment, I must confess that these famous brides and grooms seemed to lend credibility to the establishments and, although I hate to admit it, perhaps even swayed our decision. After all, if it was good enough for JFK, well, it was good enough us!

My own wedding planning experience was the inspiration for this book. Equally inspiring is my position as the public relations manager for an historic Southern California hotel. In dealing with the media on a day-to-day basis, many ask which famous people have been guests. It seems as if America has an obsession with the rich and famous, spawning numerous magazines and television shows throughout the years.

In conducting research for this book, I conducted site visits to countless hotels and inns, and spent many hours scouring archival records at the Margaret Herrick Library located at the Academy of Motion Pictures, Arts and Sciences complex in Los Angeles. I also turned to various state tourism offices, convention and visitors bureaus as well as publicists who could further assist in the cause. The information I received was overwhelming and, while I would have liked to included everyone, space and time were of the essence.

With a project of this magnitude, the final product cannot be credited to the author alone. I would like to recognize those who assisted in the process: my parents, Dan and Freddie Arrighi, who spent as much time as me - if not more - buried knee-deep in research; by brother, Steven Arrighi, who put me in touch with some of Hollywood's movers and shakers; Camille Smith, for her expertise in editing copy; my employer, the historic Queen Mary, for allowing flexibility in my schedule; and, of course, my publisher and editor, Jonathan Stein, for giving me the opportunity to write my first book. But most of all, I wish to thank my husband, Kurt Borsting, who assisted in every step of the way and, by proposing marriage, made this book possible!